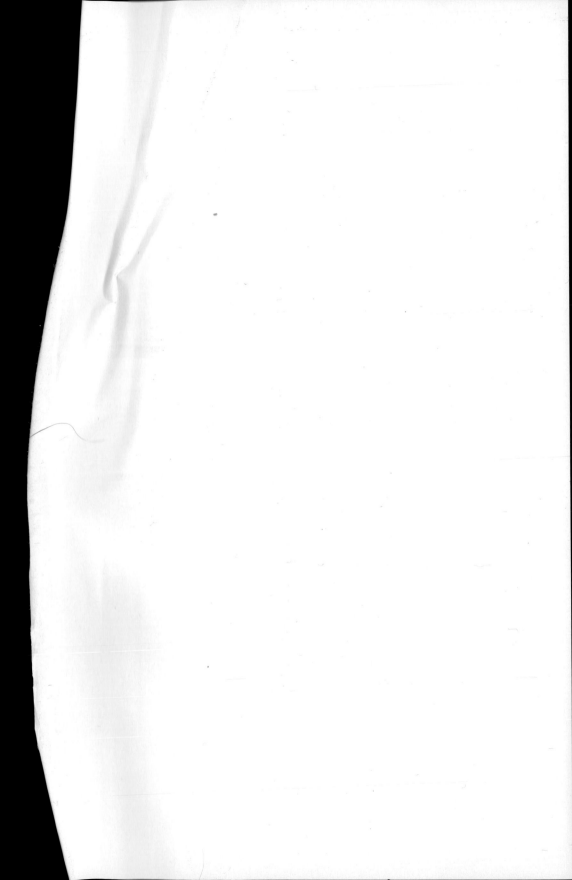

Accounts,
Accounting and Accountability

Accounts, Accounting and Accountability

Essays in memory of Peter Bird

G. MACDONALD AND
B.A. RUTHERFORD

International

Van Nostrand Reinhold
(International)

The Institute of
Chartered Accountants
in England and Wales

First published in 1989 by
Van Nostrand Reinhold (International) Co. Ltd
11 New Fetter Lane, London EC4P 4EE
and The Institute of Chartered Accountants in England and Wales,
Chartered Accountant's Hall, Moorgate Place, London EC2P 2BJ

Typeset in 11/13pt Plantin by Leaper & Gard Ltd, Bristol
Printed in Great Britain at the University Press, Cambridge

ISBN 0-7476-0036-8

British Library Cataloguing in Publication Data

Macdonald, G.
    Accounts, accounting and accountability.
    1. Accounting
    I. Title II. Rutherford, B.A. (Brian A)
    III. Bird, Peter, *1934–1987*
    657

    ISBN 0-7476-0036-8

Contents

Contents

List of contributors

1. JOHN ARNOLD
   Peat Marwick McLintock Professor of Accounting
   University of Manchester

2. W.T. BAXTER
   Emeritus Professor of Accounting
   London School of Economics and Political Science

3. MICHAEL BROMWICH
   CIMA Professor of Accounting and Financial Management
   London School of Economics and Political Science

4. HAROLD C. EDEY
   Emeritus Professor of Accounting
   London School of Economics and Political Science

5. DON HANSON
   Managing Partner
   Arthur Andersen & Co.

6. GRAEME MACDONALD
   Reader in Accounting and Taxation
   University of Kent at Canterbury

7. R.H. PARKER
   Professor of Accountancy
   University of Exeter

8. B.A. RUTHERFORD
   Professor of Accounting
   University of Kent at Canterbury

9. CLIVE M. SCHMITTHOFF
   Honorary Professor of Law
   University of Kent at Canterbury

10. GEOFFREY WHITTINGTON
    Price Waterhouse Professor of Financial Accounting
    University of Cambridge

11. ROBERT WILLOTT
    Partner
    Spicer & Oppenheim

12. SIR BRYAN CARSBERG
    Director-General
    The Office of Telecommunications
    Visiting Professor
    London School of Economics and Political Science

Preface

PETER BIRD

This collection of papers is published as a tribute to Peter Bird who, until his untimely death in April 1987, was Professor of Accounting at the University of Kent at Canterbury.

Peter graduated from the London School of Economics in 1956 with first class honours and qualified as a chartered accountant with Arthur Andersen & Co., gaining prizes in the Institute examinations. He returned to the LSE in 1963 as a lecturer in accounting, and in 1966 moved to the University of Kent to establish the Accounting Department. He was elected to a personal chair in 1970.

Throughout his academic career Peter's main interest was in financial reporting, an interest which enabled him to combine academic research with a practical contribution to the accountancy profession. Intellectual breadth and clarity of reasoning combined with humility and tolerance made him an excellent communicator with both students and practitioners. His writings were not aimed solely at his fellow academics, and his co-operation with practitioners was a feature of his work which remains an example to all academics. He served the accountancy profession as an elected member of the Council of The Institute of Chartered Accountants in England and Wales, as President of its South Eastern Society, as a member of its Technical Committee and its Research Committee, and as a member and chairman of various education and examination committees of the accountancy bodies. In so doing he also served the academic community.

His major work, *Accountability: Standards in Financial Reporting*, is still as topical, and its insights as pertinent, as when published in 1973. His lucid and unpretentious style made his writings accessible to students, academics and practitioners alike. His introductory book, *Understanding Company Accounts*, provided a clear but not simplistic guide to the uninitiated, while his contributions to *Palmer's Company Law* and the *Journal of Business Law* admirably unravelled the mysteries and problems of accounting practice for company lawyers. Peter was unconcerned with vogue. It was typical that his long-term interest in financial reporting for non-profit-seeking organizations, which resulted in the publication in 1981 (with Peter Morgan-Jones) of the research study *Financial Reporting by Charities*, should considerably pre-date the recent interest shown by academics and practitioners in the subject.

This collection represents the desire of friends and colleagues to honour the memory of an academic accountant who was admired and respected by academics and practitioners alike, both profession-ally and personally. The contributors have all worked with Peter in one or more capacity – either as teacher, student, academic colleague or fellow member of a professional committee. All, however, would like to remember him as a friend, so, although these essays clearly recognize Peter's life and work as an academic accountant, they are also contributed as a tribute to Peter the man, a past friend.

MGM
BAR
Canterbury

Selected bibliography

Bird, P.A. (9 January 1965) Waiting for the accounts, *The Accountant*, 34–6.

Bird, P.A. (Spring 1965) Tax incentives to capital investment, *Journal of Accounting Research*, 3 : 1, 1–11.

Bird, P.A. (November–December 1965) The incorporation of small businesses: effects of the Finance Act 1965, *The British Tax Review*, pp. 393–401.

Bird, P.A. (10 June 1967) The audit of university expenditure, *The Accountant*, pp. 763–5.

Bird, P.A. (Winter 1970) The scope of the company audit, *Accounting and Business Research*, 1 : 1, 44–9.

Bird, P.A. (ed.) (1971) *A Casebook on Auditing Procedures*, 2nd edn., Institute of Chartered Accountants in England and Wales, London.

Bird, P.A. (1971) *The Interpretation of Published Accounts*, HMSO, London.

Bird, P.A. (1973) *Accountability: Standards in Financial Reporting*, Accountancy Age Books, London.

Bird, P.A. (Spring 1973) What is capital gearing? *Accounting and Business Research*, 3 : 10, 92–7.

Bird, P.A. (1974) Standard accounting practice, in *Debits, Credits, Finance and Profits*, H. Edey and B.S. Yamey (eds), Sweet and Maxwell, London.

Bird, P.A. (Summer 1975) Objectives and methods of financial reporting: a generalized search procedure, *Accounting and Business Research*, 5 : 19, 162–7.

Bird, P.A. (1981) Research issues in accounting for non-business organizations, in *Essays in British Accounting Research*, M. Bromwich and A. Hopwood (eds), Pitman, London.

Bird, P.A. (June 1982) After Argyll Foods what is a 'true and fair view'? *Accountancy*, 94 : 1065, 80–1.

Bird, P.A. (September 1982) Group accounts and the true and fair view, *Journal of Business Law*, pp. 364–8.

Bird, P.A. (1983) *Understanding Company Accounts*, 2nd edn., Pitman, London.

Bird, P.A. (1984) Charity accounts, in *Financial Reporting 1984–85: A Survey of UK Published Accounts*, Institute of Chartered Accountants in England and Wales, London.

Bird, P.A. (1984) The complexities of simplified accounts, in *External Financial Reporting*, B. Carsberg and S. Dev (eds), Prentice-Hall, London.

Bird, P.A. (1984) The development of standard accounting practice, in *Current Issues in Accounting*, B. Carsberg and A. Hope (eds), Philip Allan, Oxford.

Bird, P.A. (November 1984) What is a 'true and fair view'? *Journal of Business Law*, pp. 480–5.

Bird, P.A. (Winter 1985) The level of reserves in fund-raising charities, *Financial Accountability and Management*, 1 : 2, 161–72.

Bird, P.A. and Jackson, C.I. (March 1966) The water cure, *British Waterworks Association Journal*, XLVIII : 414, pp. 171–8.

Bird, P.A. and Jackson, C.I. (June 1966) Public utility or social service, *Town and Country Planning*, XXXIV : 6, pp. 332–4.

Bird, P.A. and Jackson, C.I. (1967) Economic charges for water, in *Essays in the Theory and Practice of Pricing*, Institute of Economic Affairs, London.

Bird, P.A. and Jackson, C.I. (March 1967) Water supply: the transformation of an industry, *The Three Banks Review*, pp. 3–15.

Bird, P.A. and Thirlwall, A.P. (June 1967) The incentive to invest in the new Development Areas, *District Bank Review*

Bird, P.A. and Morgan-Jones, P. (1981) *Financial Reporting by Charities*, Institute of Chartered Accountants in England and Wales, London.

Bird, P.A. and Morris, R.C. (1987) Part 8: Accounts, audit and dividends, in *Palmer's Company Law*, 24th edn., Stevens, London.

Bird, P.A., Macdonald, G. and Climo, T. (1975) *Statements of Objectives and Standard Practice in Financial Reporting*, Accountancy Age Books, London.

1

Accounting education and research: the role of universities

JOHN ARNOLD

INTRODUCTION

There are presently some 130 000 professionally qualified accountants in the UK working in practice, industry and commerce in both
the private and the public sector. University accounting departments
have a role to play in contributing to the effectiveness with which
these accountants undertake their various tasks. University departments have the potential to influence accountants and accounting in
a number of ways. They may provide initial education to those
intending to train as accountants and to the trainees themselves.
They may provide continuing education to those who have already
qualified. They may undertake research which will influence other
educators (and hence the intending and actual accountants they are
teaching), accountants, and those − such as regulators − who are
interested in accountants and accountancy.

In this paper, we first consider the purposes of university departments of accounting. We next explore in some detail the education
and training of accountants and the nature and role of accounting
research. We then attempt to pull together the various strands by
considering existing and potential relationships between research,
education and practice. Our conclusions are that university accounting departments in the United Kingdom have considerable untapped

potential both to educate accountants and to provide relevant research for and about accountants.*

THE PURPOSES OF UNIVERSITY DEPARTMENTS OF ACCOUNTING

Departments of accounting (and finance) in universities are one arm of the accountancy profession. In order to understand their role and to identify the areas in which they might enjoy comparative advantages over other parts of the profession, it is important to understand their purposes. Broadly these depend on the aims and objectives of the universities of which accounting departments are a part. The overriding objective of most universities is the creation and dissemination of knowledge. This is achieved through the two main activities of universities – teaching and research. In accounting both are (or should be) of interest to the practising arm of the profession.

(a) Teaching

In common with many other vocational subjects such as law and engineering, the main teaching objective of university accounting departments is to provide students with a conceptual framework and theoretical underpinning of the subject in order to enhance their understanding of practice and to develop their ability to contribute beneficially to future changes in practice. The teaching of current practice itself is usually restricted to a coverage of the amount which is necessary to make sense of the theoretical underpinning. The emphasis is on the instillation of a critical (in the constructive sense) attitude to accounting and accountants. Detailed teaching of practice, or 'training', is recognized as being best left to practitioners.

---

*Much of what is said in the paper applies with equal force to accounting departments in polytechnics. However, there are significant differences. For example, polytechnic teachers, unlike their university counterparts, have no contractual obligation to undertake research, although some do. Because of the difference, the analysis in this paper is for the most part restricted to university departments.

(b) Research

Collins English Dictionary defines research as: 'systematic investigation to establish facts or principles or to collect information on a subject'. Accounting research involves the collection and analysis of 'facts', the development of principles, the collection of information concerning accounting statements of all kinds, the uses to which that information is put and the role and behaviour of accountants and those who are affected by the information they provide. Within this rather broad description the emphasis in university departments, as with teaching, is on areas which would not be likely to be undertaken, or to be undertaken to an adequate extent, by industrial and commercial firms, including the professional accountancy firms. So, for example, 'blue-sky' research, which is concerned with the investigation of problems and phenomena which have no immediate practical application and is often highly speculative, is more appropriately undertaken in universities than in commercial firms. The results of such research are often beneficial to the community as a whole rather than to one particular firm. Thus it cannot be left to individual private sector organizations, with profit-orientated goals, to undertake such research to a socially optimal level. This problem is discussed further in the section on research.

(c) Scholarship

As part of the environment necessary for them to undertake high-quality teaching and research, university staff are provided with the opportunity to read, think and study which is rarely available to the same extent to their professional colleagues. This ability to take a longer-term view of problems, unencumbered by the need to find an immediate practical solution, is one of the major advantages enjoyed by academics and one which enables them to offer unique contributions to the development of accountancy.

EDUCATION AND TRAINING*

In this section the role of university departments in the education and training of accountants is considered. The proper education and

*This section draws heavily on Arnold (1986).

training of accountants is a matter of concern both to the accountants themselves and to those for whom they work and provide services. Although post-qualification education and training is of great importance, the contribution of universities at present is primarily to pre-qualification arrangements. This section will, in consequence, be directed mostly to those arrangements.

As a prelude it is necessary to ask what sort of person should a newly qualified accountant be. That is not an easy question to answer. Our view is that, because so many qualified accountants eventually pursue careers in business management, the newly qualified should possess a range of general business skills. An alternative view is that the emphasis should be on competence in accounting. As accounting is concerned with the provision of financial information for decision-making, planning and control, and as those activities frequently take place in a commercial environment, the latter view implies at least some awareness of the business world. The difference between the two views is primarily a matter of emphasis, but it is an important difference because of the finite amount of time which is available for pre-qualification education and training in practice. It is not feasible in the time available to provide a comprehensive education and training in both general business skills and accounting. Faced with the choice, accounting educators and trainers should probably do what they are best at and concentrate on the instillation of accounting skills.

(a) The skills and abilities required of an accountant

The accountant's environment has changed rapidly in the past decade or so and is likely to continue to do so. In consequence, a major quality which the education and training process should seek to provide is the ability to adapt. If the accountant is to continue to play a significant role in the UK economy he must be able to contribute to the achievement of dynamic efficiency (i.e. the facility to adapt and react to change) as well as to static efficiency (i.e. the ability to handle resources presently available).

So what skills and abilities does the accountant of the late twentieth century need? It is helpful to distinguish between skills which should have been acquired by all accountants at initial qualifi-

4

cation and skills which relate to post-qualification specialization and which may therefore be acquired after qualification. The former group may be thought of as core skills which are relevant for all subsequent specializations and the latter as specialist skills, the need for which will depend on the particular route followed by the accountant after initial qualification. Amongst the specialist skills might be included personnel management, marketing skills and leadership skills which will become important to many accountants as they progress upwards in organizations but which are not all essential to every accountant.

Core skills on the other hand provide a bench-mark against which alternative systems of pre-qualification education and training may be evaluated. It should be self-evident that they include basic skills in numeracy and literacy which should have been acquired during primary and secondary education. What additional skills are then necessary prior to qualification? First, in order to appreciate the current potential contribution of accounting, the accountant must understand what accounting is at present and be able to evaluate its strengths and weaknesses. For this he needs both technical knowledge (i.e. knowledge about current practices, standards and legal requirements) and analytical skills, including the ability to synthesize and evaluate critically. In order to contribute to the achievement of dynamic efficiency he must also be able to judge when and how change is needed to current accounting practices. For this he must possess additional attributes. He must understand the conceptual foundation underlying present practice; in other words, he needs a knowledge of the situations and circumstances in which present practice is and is not appropriate and of the assumptions, principles and objectives upon which it is based. Furthermore, in order to acquire the skills necessary to evaluate both existing practice and future needs, he will need to possess a certain level of intellectual ability and maturity. Finally, if the accountant is to be effective in the implementation of change, he must be capable of convincing others to adopt his recommendations. In order to achieve this aim, he requires communication skills and, if he is to maintain his credibility as a professional, ethical standards.

Thus a newly qualified accountant should possess technical knowledge, analytical skills, conceptual understanding, intellectual ability and maturity, communications skills and ethical standards. Many of these qualities will need to be maintained and developed, together with other more specialist skills, after initial qualification by a structured programme of post-qualification education and training. It is outside the scope of this paper to explore this particular avenue in detail. However, its importance is an increasing function of the rate of environmental change; accounting is a dynamic discipline operating in a rapidly changing environment and to assume that the qualities possessed at qualification will be adequate throughout a professional career is clearly nonsense.

(b) The present system

Each of the six UK professional accountancy bodies has its own system of education and training, between which there are significant similarities. The Institute of Chartered Accountants in England and Wales will be used in this section to illustrate the approach adopted by the largest of the bodies. It has some 70000 members in the UK (more than all the other bodies combined), and its members recruit into training contracts over 10% of all UK university graduates each year. Nevertheless, many of the arguments apply with equal force to the other bodies.

There are three main routes to qualification, each of which comprises a period of foundation education followed by a period of professional education and training:

1. The *accounting graduate* spends three years studying for his degree, which satisfies the foundation education requirement to provide a 'sound and appropriate base for the studies, training and work experience leading to qualification' (ICAEW, 1985). Professional education and training is then acquired during a three-year training contract period in an approved training office, and assessed by two professional examinations, the first of which is normally taken some fifteen months into the training contract and the second just over a year later, and by the completion of approved training. The professional examinations are set by the Institute and students normally prepare for the examinations by attending courses run by private sector tutorial organiz-

ations. Such courses last a total of approximately ten weeks for
each of the professional examinations;

2. The *non-accounting graduate* spends three years studying for his
   degree. He satisfies the foundation education requirement by
   attendance at an approved conversion course during the first six
   to nine months of his training contract. The course is taught and
   examined by one of the private sector tutorial organizations and
   involves approximately eight to ten weeks of attendance. He
   subsequently completes his professional education and training
   following the same pattern as the accounting graduate, but
   taking the examinations six months later to allow for the delay
   in starting professional studies caused by the need to attend a
   conversion course;

3. The *foundation course student* completes foundation education
   by attending an approved nine-month course at a polytechnic.
   He then enters a four-year training contract and satisfies the
   requirements for professional education and training within the
   same general framework as the graduate but usually at a slower
   pace.

Details of the numbers opting for each of the three routes
between 1977 and 1986/87 are given in Table 1.1. The number of
accounting graduates signing training contracts has grown slowly
from almost 1000 to something over 1200 each year, representing
some 20% of the total intake. The annual intake of non-accounting
graduates has increased from 2000 (43%) in 1977 to 4300 (69%) in
1986/87 while foundation course entrants have fallen over the same
period from 1500 (32%) to 500 (8%). The trend is clearly towards an
increasing percentage of graduates and, in particular, of non-
accounting graduates.

One thread common to all routes is that most accounting
education is provided by private sector organizations rather than by
university and polytechnic accounting departments. All tuition for
the professional examinations is in the private sector as is the provision of foundation education in the basic disciplines for non-
accounting graduates, who currently represent some 70% of the
total intake. That is a situation which is unique in the developed
world.

Table 1.1 Original entry to training contracts 1977–1986/87.

	UK accounting graduates	UK non-accounting graduates	Foundation course students	Other	Total
1977	894	2024	1482	283	4683
	(19%)	(43%)	(32%)	(6%)	(100%)
1978	985	2365	1343	280	4973
	(20%)	(48%)	(27%)	(5%)	(100%)
1979	1064	2598	1098	316	5076
	(21%)	(51%)	(22%)	(6%)	(100%)
1980	1149	2961	898	256	5264
	(22%)	(56%)	(17%)	(5%)	(100%)
1981	1098	2852	807	172	4929
	(22%)	(58%)	(16%)	(4%)	(100%)
1982	1061	2744	735	131	4671
	(22%)	(59%)	(16%)	(3%)	(100%)
1983	1100	3040	621	98	4859
	(23%)	(62%)	(13%)	(2%)	(100%)
1984	1117	3455	517	82	5171
	(21%)	(67%)	(10%)	(2%)	(100%)
1985	1268	4323	536	149	6276
	(20%)	(69%)	(9%)	(2%)	(100%)
1986/87	1246	4342	526	173	6287
	(20%)	(69%)	(8%)	(3%)	(100%)

Derived from ICAEW (1988).

(c) How successful is the present system?

On the face of it, the present system is very successful. The English Institute admits some 3000 new members each year and the demand for chartered accountants is buoyant, as is evident from the high salaries currently being offered. However, it would be both naïve and complacent to conclude from this that all is well with existing education and training arrangements. There are aspects of the present system which offer considerable opportunity for improvement.

Consider first the extent to which the present system succeeds in imparting the skills and abilities required of a newly qualified accountant. There are two types of evidence which might be used to evaluate the extent to which today's accountants possess appropriate skills and abilities. Both are somewhat imprecise and speculative and depend in part on the exercise of individual judgement and opinion. The first is the observed performance of accountants as reflected by the demand for their services and their ability to handle new and emerging problems (i.e. measures of the quality of the *output* of the education and training process). The second is the type and quality of instruction which is provided during the period of education and training (i.e. the quality of the *input*).

There is plentiful evidence that the market demand for accountants and their services is high. One reason for this could be the high quality of the intake of trainee accountants. The quality of the newly qualified chartered accountant is a function of both the quality of the person entering accounting education and training and of the quality of the education and training itself.

Furthermore, some recent examples suggest that the quality of the output is less high than it might be. The first is the accountancy profession's response to the numerous changes already created by developments in information technology. In general, the response has been swift. The profession has succeeded in carving out for itself a substantial corner of the market for information technology services. However, credit for this can hardly be claimed for the current professional education process; information technology has not featured as an important part of the professional examination syllabuses and, in consequence, has not been taught by the private sector tutors. (That situation is now changing with the introduction of new syllabuses – see ICAEW (1985).) A more likely explanation is that professional accountancy firms perceived a potential market demand and met it by recruiting information technology experts and using them to train existing staff. The danger is that the creation of 'instant experts' may not provide a very solid base for future evolution and development. The information technology area is still relatively new and, in the short term at least, a limited expertise may be sufficient to beat the competition. In the longer term, the most successful in this area are likely to be those possessing a thorough conceptual understanding and training in information technology. It remains to be seen whether they will be accountants.

A second example of an area where accountants have not been particularly successful is in the setting of accounting standards. It is possible that the lack of a clear understanding of the conceptual foundation underlying existing practice and an appreciation of the assumptions, principles and objectives upon which alternative treatments are based, together with, in particular, a failure to recognize the importance of economic and political consequences, were major factors in the inflation accounting débâcle as well as in the problems surrounding merger accounting, accounting for associated companies, goodwill, brand names, foreign currency translation, the treatment of long-term contract work in progress and off balance sheet finance.

Consider now the input to the education process and, in particular, the relative contributions of university (and polytechnic) departments on the one hand and private sector tutors on the other. Each enjoys comparative advantages in the provision of the skills and abilities required of accountants. Academic accountants normally possess higher degrees in accounting (as well as, for most, professional qualifications) and operate in an environment where the emphasis is on analytical skills and conceptual understanding.

Private sector tutors often have different backgrounds and work in a very different environment. They compete in a market where success in preparing students for the Institute's professional examinations is perhaps the most important factor in their ability to retain existing clients and attract new ones. In consequence, the content of their courses is heavily influenced by the professional examination syllabuses which have historically tended to reflect the practical rather than the conceptual aspects of accountancy. In order to teach such courses, the private sector tutorial organizations have recruited staff with particular strengths in current practices, standards and legal requirements, i.e. staff who enjoy a comparative advantage in the teaching of technical knowledge. Furthermore, private sector organizations work more closely with their professional firm clients than do university or polytechnic departments, which tends to reinforce their emphasis on current practice.

Thus on balance, academic accountants enjoy a comparative advantage in, and might consequently be expected to bear primary responsibility for, the teaching of conceptual and analytical skills while private sector tutors have the edge in, and should probably be primarily responsible for, the teaching of technical knowledge. In so far as the other necessary skills are concerned, there seems to be no comparative advantage for either type of teacher. Intellectual ability and maturity is the product of a sound general education and is likely to be developed in both types of organization. Communication skills and ethical standards are capable of being acquired in both the education and training stages of the process.

To what extent does the current situation match the one suggested? The earlier description of the present system reveals that for accounting graduates it matches quite closely and it might be expected that newly qualified accountants who also possess an accounting degree are better equipped, in terms of basic skills, to cope with a dynamic environment than are their non-accounting graduate contemporaries for whom the present system matches the suggested one less closely. The latter group receives broadly the same education for the professional examinations as do the former. But conversion courses, which are the primary vehicle for education in conceptual understanding for non-accounting graduates, involve only eight to ten weeks of tuition, a much shorter time than is provided to accounting graduates. However, the view that accounting graduates are better equipped than non-accounting graduates is frequently contested by those who argue that the statistics show that accounting graduates do 'less well' in their professional examinations. Such an argument is false for two reasons.

The first is that the professional examinations have not in the past tested the full range of skills which, it has been argued, are necessary for the newly qualified accountant and have instead been primarily a test of technical knowledge, in which accounting graduates might be expected to have no particular relative advantage. Furthermore, success in the professional examinations may not be a particularly good indicator of a trainee's ability to make a success of a subsequent professional career.

The second reason is that excessive concentration on the 'bottom line' of a set of statistics is almost as misleading as similar concentration on the bottom line of an income statement! Consider Table 1.2 which contains various statistics relating to success in the final professional examination (PEII) during 1987. The first line does

Table 1.2 Successful graduate candidates (first attempt or referred at first attempt) for PEII examination sessions in 1987.

	Accounting graduates	*Non-accounting graduates*
Overall pass rate	47.3%	54.2%
Overall pass rate, excluding Oxbridge and polytechnic candidates	53.9%	52.0%
Pass rates by degree class:		
I and II(i):		
University (excluding Oxbridge)	67.3%	61.2%
Polytechnic	51.4%	40.0%
II(ii):		
University (excluding Oxbridge)	41.8%	44.1%
Polytechnic	19.2%	26.0%
III and Pass:		
University (excluding Oxbridge)	29.8%	35.3%
Polytechnic	23.7%	18.2%

Derived from ICAEW (1988).

indeed show that non-accounting graduates overall enjoyed a higher rate of success than did accounting graduates. But this global statistic hides other important features. It includes Oxbridge graduates, who all have non-accounting degrees and who perform significantly better than do non-Oxbridge graduates. It includes CNAA (polytechnic) graduates, the vast majority of whom possess accounting degrees and who perform significantly worse than do university graduates. Finally, it ignores the class of degree achieved. Removing

Oxbridge and polytechnic graduates shows accounting graduates performing marginally better than non-accounting degree holders. Further analysis by degree class for non-Oxbridge university and polytechnic graduates is equally revealing. Holders of first and upper second class accounting degrees performed noticeably better than their non-accounting counterparts. The performance of lower second class degree holders was broadly similar for accounting and non-accounting graduates. Third class and pass accounting degree holders did less well than equivalent non-accounting graduates. It would not be wise to attempt to generalize from one year's figures and the preceding analysis is offered primarily as an illustration of the dangers of excessive concentration on one statistic. Nevertheless, the same pattern is evident for the first professional examination results in 1987 and for the few other years for which statistics are available.

In addition to its shortcomings in providing newly qualified accountants with the full range of skills and abilities which they are likely to need, the present system of professional education and training is less efficient than it might be in at least one other respect. Very little credit is given to accounting graduates in respect of their university studies. For example, in the case of The Institute of Chartered Accountants in England and Wales, accounting graduates receive exemption only from the initial conversion course of graduates. At present they receive no reduction in their overall training period. This seems at least an ungenerous recognition of the completion of an approved three-year accounting course.

(d) Scope for improvement?

Although much of the preceding analysis has been illustrated in the context of The Institute of Chartered Accountants in England and Wales, the criticisms raised may, in most cases, be levelled also at the other five professional bodies. Specifically, there is scope for the professional bodies to make more use of the resources available in universities and polytechnics to improve both the effectiveness of the education of accountants (i.e. the extent to which it achieves its objectives of imparting necessary abilities and skills) and its efficiency (i.e. the cost at which stated objectives are achieved).

RESEARCH

In this section the nature of accounting research is discussed, together with the relative contributions of university departments and academics and professional firms and bodies. Accounting research involves both the collection of information concerning accountants and accounting and the development of principles. It includes the study of a wide range of topics including financial accounting and reporting, auditing, management and management accounting, financial management, finance and taxation. Each of these topics may be studied in the private or public sectors, and nationally or internationally. They may be investigated at different levels and using a variety of research methods. They may also be studied from different perspectives – in particular from the point of view of the accountant with a problem to solve or from the point of view of another party wishing to observe the behaviour of accountants and its consequences.

In order to examine the role and relevance of research it is useful to explore some of these differences further.

(a) Levels of research

SSAP 13 (on research and development) distinguishes between pure (or basic) research, applied research and development. The definitions given may be modified slightly to describe different types of accounting research.

Basic accounting research is original investigation undertaken in order to gain new knowledge and understanding. Basic accounting research is not primarily directed towards any specific practical aim or application. Broadly speaking, the results of basic accounting research are likely to be of most immediate interest to scholars of accounting who wish to understand its historical development and its current role and context. However, in the longer run the results are likely to provide the basis for applied work.

Applied accounting research is original investigation undertaken in order to gain new knowledge and directed towards a specific practical aim or objective. The results of such research will probably be of interest to those practising accounting in all its forms and to those affected by accounting practice, as well as to scholars of accounting. The benefits of the research are unlikely to be exclusive to a particular organization.

Accounting development is the use of knowledge in order to produce new or substantially improved procedures, systems or services. Its results are likely to interest the particular organizations which sponsor or undertake the work and which may be able, at least in the short term, to enjoy the benefits without sharing them with other organizations.

(b) Research methods

Accounting theories may be categorized broadly as either normative (prescriptive) or positive (descriptive). Normative theories are concerned with what ought to be, and positive theories with what actually happens. It follows that normative theories are based largely on value judgements, whereas positive theories are not. This distinction is important in the selection of the research methods to be used to examine particular theories. A rich variety of research methods is now used in accounting research (Sundem, 1977). Most are either analytical or empirical.

Analytical methods usually involve the construction of a model from assumed or observed relationships, from which a conclusion or a set of conclusions is logically deduced. Such models, which in accounting may be in the form of verbal expressions, geometric diagrams or mathematical expressions, are the means by which both normative and positive theories are described.

Empirical methods are used to test positive theories, by comparing the results predicted by the model with what is observed to happen in the real world. Normative theories cannot be tested empirically because they are not intended to predict actual outcomes. Empirical data may be obtained from available sources such as databases of published accounting information and share prices, or they may be collected directly by the researcher, for example by questionnaire survey, interview or observation.

(c) Alternative perspectives

Traditionally, much accounting research has been concerned with an examination of the information which accountants produce, both for use within and outside organizations, and in particular with making recommendations for improving the 'quality' of that information. Demski (1987) has described this approach as:

> ... the temptation to pontificate. Our task is not, in a social science perspective, to tell our professional counterparts what to do. They are specialized in action. Researchers are specialized in observation. (p. 94)

Demski's description reflects a move in accounting research, during the past decade or so, away from normative research into the problems which face accountants, towards positive research into what accountants do and what the implications are of their procedures and actions for other parts of society. This change in perspective, which might be (slightly unfairly) categorized as a move away from attempting to solve problems facing accountants towards attempting to identify problems caused by accountants and accounting, may explain the frustration of practitioners with much current academic research which they perceive, largely correctly, as being of limited short-term benefit to them.

The role of and responsibility for accounting research are now considered in the light of the different levels, methods and perspectives discussed above.

(d) The role of accounting research

A major purpose of accounting research ultimately is to contribute to the solution of practical problems by enhancing our understanding of their causes and consequences. Such problems may be those faced by accountants or those caused by accountants or accounting. Research into the problems faced by accountants should eventually benefit accountants by contributing to the solution of those problems. Research into the problems caused by accountants or accounting is likely to produce results of interest to those who have to work with accountants and those who regulate their activities.

So the role of accounting research is wide and extends beyond the solution of (short-term) problems of immediate concern to accountants themselves. An expectation that all accounting research will produce short- and medium-term benefits for accountants or the accountancy profession thus represents a misunderstanding of the purposes and potential of such research. Some of the benefits will be long term. Others will not accrue to the accountancy profession at all.

(e) Who should undertake (and fund) accounting research?

The academic accountant is (or should be) both reactive and innovative. As a reactor, he should undertake research and scholarship to learn about the current state of accounting as it is practised and communicate that knowledge to students and other interested parties. The innovative role is crucial; without it, accounting practice would fail to develop or react to environmental changes. Of course, innovations in accounting are not the sole preserve of academics. Many accountancy firms and other business organizations have excellent technical and research departments. Nevertheless, academics are particularly advantageously placed to take a long-term view of the subject and to devote time to a study of its underlying concepts and principles. Indeed, a substantial part of the annual government grant to universities is specifically intended to fund such research. Perhaps, then, the question should not be who should undertake accounting research but rather who should fund it.

The answer to this question will depend on both the level of research (basic, applied or development) and on the perspective adopted (is it to help accountants or those who are interested in the behaviour of accountants and accounting?). In general, the costs of research will, in a capitalist economy, be borne by those who benefit from it.

Consider first the perspective. Research which is designed to help accountants should, in general, be funded by individual firms or by professional bodies, depending on its level. The funding of research about accountants and accountancy is less clear. Who derives the benefits from such research? In so far as the regulation of the behaviour of accountants is of interest to society at large, then society (through agencies such as the University Grants Committee and the Economic and Social Research Council, which are funded by the Government) should support the research. On the other hand, the accountancy profession in the United Kingdom is largely self-regulated. In so far as the profession wishes to continue to regulate itself, it might be expected to bear the cost of some of the research into its role in and impact on society. (This may be a somewhat risky strategy of course, if the research suggests that self-regulation is not in the best interests of the rest of UK society!)

Responsibility for funding will depend also on the level of the research. There is little incentive for individual firms or even particular industrial or professional sectors to fund basic (or pure) research. The benefits are long term, sometimes speculative and widely spread and if one firm alone incurs the cost it is unlikely that the benefits to the firm will be sufficient to justify the cost. For that reason, basic research in accounting (as in many other subjects) is often funded by the government. In accounting, such funding comes primarily from the University Grants Committee and the Economic and Social Research Council. During the past five years or so, the funds available to both bodies have been cut in real terms. This reflects implicitly the government's view of the social benefits of basic research. It also raises the possibility that the accountancy bodies, as part of their obligation as learned professional bodies, should attempt to make good some of the deficit.

Applied accounting research will normally produce results which are of value to the accountancy profession as a whole, but, because the benefits are unlikely to be exclusive to one particular organization, there is generally little incentive for any individual firm to fund it. It is an area where there is an obvious need for the professional accountancy bodies to provide support on behalf of their members.

Accounting development, or technical work, will often provide benefits which are peculiar to particular organizations at least for the short term. In consequence, it is reasonable to expect the organizations which benefit from the research to fund it up to the level where the marginal benefits from the research are just equal to the marginal costs of undertaking it.

The above analysis suggests broadly that the government should fund basic accounting research and at least some of the research which investigates the role and influence of accountancy in society. The professional accountancy bodies should probably also fund some of this latter type of research together with applied research which is designed to help their members. Individual firms should fund development work which is designed to solve problems which they face.

In practice, the picture is not so clear. Differences between categories of levels and perspectives of research are sometimes blurred. Furthermore, if government funding of basic research and research into the role of accountancy in society is perceived (by accountants?) as being inadequate, it may be appropriate for the professional accountancy bodies to fund some or all of the perceived shortfall. Such action may contribute to the preservation of the professional reputations of their members and would be consistent with the objectives of these bodies. For example, the first principal objective of The Institute of Chartered Accountants in England and Wales is 'to advance the theory and practice of accountancy in all its aspects, including in particular auditing, financial management and taxation' (Supplemental Charter of 1948).

THE RELATIONSHIP BETWEEN RESEARCH, EDUCATION AND PRACTICE

The relationship between research, education and practice in accounting often seems to be different from what it is in other disciplines. Sterling (1973) has characterized it as follows:

$$P(x) \rightarrow E(x) \rightarrow P(x) \tag{1.1}$$

In words, the educators teach x (E(x)) because that is what is practised (P(x)) and, as a result, those who have been 'educated' go out and practise x. This is clearly a means of perpetuating current practice and of stifling innovation. Furthermore, there is no place for research in the model. In this section, the validity of Sterling's model (together with his alternative normative model) will be discussed, and suggestions will be made for bringing closer together the actual situation in accounting in the UK with the desired state.

19

(a) A normative model

Sterling's model of how things ought to be in accounting (and of how they often are in other disciplines) is:

$$R(x) \to E(x) \to P(x) \qquad (1.2)$$

In words, if research shows x to be the case $(R(x))$, x is taught by educators and students eventually implement x in practice. Sterling's model is perhaps an oversimplified representation of the ways things ought to be in accounting, for at least two reasons:

1. It ignores the interaction which ought to exist between research and practice. At least some accounting research should be concerned with describing and explaining practice. It also fails to reflect the dynamic nature of the process by which research and education should influence practice and changes in practice should influence research and consequently education. Hence we might expect to see a feedback loop in the model from practice back to research.
2. It is unclear what is meant in the model by accounting education. Sterling's model relates to a world in which education is provided, at an educational institution, prior to practice being undertaken. In UK accounting, education is usually followed and/or accompanied by professional training. In addition, continuing professional education (CPE) is provided both in the form of courses and by articles in journals which are read by accountants.

These points suggest the need for a more complex (normative) model than that suggested by Sterling:

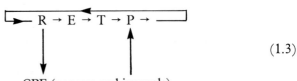

$$(1.3)$$

CPE (courses and journals)

In words, research results influence the content of educational and training courses, including CPE courses, and of journal articles, all of which influence practice. Changes in practice are then reflected in research, so that the whole process is continuous.

(b) Problems with the normative model in accounting

Unfortunately, model 1.1 above appears to be a better representation of UK accounting than model 1.3. Why should that be the case? There are a number of possible explanations, several of which have already been explored in this paper. They relate both to the *supply* of education, training and research and to the *demand* for them.

Consider first the supply of education and training. Education and training (including CPE) for the majority of professionally qualified accountants is provided exclusively by private sector tutors who themselves have no expertise in research. Their comparative advantage lies in their knowledge of current practice – in consequence, that is what they prefer to teach.

The demand for education, which usually comes from the partners and managers in practising firms on behalf of their trainees and other staff, is influenced by the content of professional examinations (which have been predominantly practical in the past) and by the perceived need for professional relevance.

An examination of the syllabuses of any of the professional accountancy bodies will show that the content of professional examinations is changing; the emphasis is less on testing whether candidates are able to reproduce current techniques and more on the understanding of underlying principles and the ability to analyse problems. It is less clear whether a majority of practitioners yet acknowledge that professional relevance is not concerned exclusively with current practice. Until they do, and until the changing nature of the professional examinations is fully recognized, the education and training skills available in university accounting departments are unlikely to be exploited to their full potential.

Research is supplied predominantly by academics. Until the last decade or so, academic accounting in the UK has been a small community with a relatively small research output. There has been relatively little accounting research available to practising accountants, although this situation is now changing. A further problem persists, however. The level of funding made available from government sources to fund basic and some applied research has been curtailed during the past seven or eight years. For the reasons explained earlier, such research might not be funded by individual firms or, in some cases, by professional associations. This has contributed to the shortage in supply of accounting research.

Consider now the demand side of the equation. Why do practising accountants not insist on acquiring more accounting research? A major problem here seems to be that they do not perceive much accounting research to be of relevance to them. Many academics have chosen to undertake quite abstract research which has little obvious immediate relevance to practice. The situation does seem to be changing with an increasing emphasis emerging on research which attempts to describe and explain current practice.

The demand for accounting research (and indeed for education and training provided by university accounting departments) may also be depressed by the way the product is marketed! The promotions structure in universities (where the vast majority of accounting research is conducted) depends heavily on research performance, of which the primary indicator is the ability of the researcher to publish in journals where manuscripts are sent for evaluation anonymously to referees, who are invariably also academics. As a result, articles in refereed journals tend to be rigorously argued and often contain quite specialized academic language, which is familiar to other academic accountants but less so to practitioners. (In this respect academic accounting is little different from accounting practice which also has a specialized and often esoteric vocabulary.) Under existing procedures for promotion in most universities there is little incentive for academics to 'translate' their work into a form of words in which it is easily accessible to practitioners. Perhaps more surprisingly, practitioners such as the technical partners of firms, have also not found it worthwhile to undertake the translation.

CONCLUSIONS

The main functions of a university are teaching, research and scholarship. In accounting departments, these functions are channelled to the provision of education in accounting and to the undertaking of accounting research. In this paper we have looked at these two areas separately and at the ways in which they interact with each other and with practice.

In each respect, we have suggested that the extant situation is far from ideal. As regards education, we argued that there is scope for the professional accountancy bodies to make more use of available resources in universities (and in polytechnics) to improve the quality of education provided to accountants. Improvements in both effectiveness and efficiency are potentially possible.

As regards research, the failure of the government to fund basic accounting research in universities adequately means that such funding must be provided in part by the accountancy profession if basic accounting research is to be undertaken to an optimal level. Despite the possible lack of economic rewards to the profession from such research, it does seem that a number of professional bodies are willing to accept this commitment.

At the interface between academe and practice, we have argued that beneficial developments are possible on both sides. Practitioners could recognize more fully the benefits of accounting education which is based on the understanding of basic principles and the development of rigorous analytical skills. Some could also acknowledge more readily the relevance of and the need for research which looks beyond today's technical problems. For their part, academics might make a greater effort to communicate more clearly both their teaching objectives and their research results to practitioners. They might also recognize that many practitioner problems do in fact provide potentially fruitful material for educational courses and research.

These conclusions are offered in a constructive spirit. It is important to recognize that enormous strides have been made during the past two decades in developing the relationship between academics and practitioners in accounting. A similar rate of progress during the next two decades would be to the mutual benefit of both groups.

REFERENCES

Arnold, J. (1986) *The Education of Accountants: At the Crossroads?* Armitage and Norton, Huddersfield.

Demski, J. (1987) (Theoretical) research in (managerial) accounting, in *Accounting and Culture*, B.E. Cushing (ed.), American Accounting Association, Sarasota, Florida.

ICAEW (1985) *New Examination Syllabuses: A Statement of Intent*, Institute of Chartered Accountants in England and Wales, London.

ICAEW (1988) *Digest of Education and Training Statistics 1986/7*, Institute of Chartered Accountants in England and Wales, London.

Sterling, R.R. (1973) Accounting research, education and practice, *Journal of Accountancy*, **136** : 3, 44–52.

Sundem, G. (1977) Overview of four years of submissions to *The Accounting Review*, **LXII** : 1, 191–202.

2

Income:
a will-o'-the-wisp?

W.T. BAXTER

I was one of Peter Bird's teachers at LSE. So his sad death naturally prompts thoughts, not only about his achievements at Canterbury, but also about his earlier days as an LSE lecturer and student; and so about his fellow students, their courses, and the teaching of those times. How far do my own old lectures now seem even more inadequate than when they were given? What bits of them have become obsolete? What new matter is needed? With such thoughts in mind, I have had another look at my lecture to undergraduates on income theory, and have tried to recast it in a way apt for today – sticking to the rule that such an introduction must be kept simple and yet must not offend against fundamentals. Here follows the result.

INTRODUCTION

Forgive me if I start by reminding you that former generations of students were happily ignorant of all ideas about income concepts. Much the same could be said of their teachers. Hatfield's *Accounting* (1927) introduces the topic, but awareness was slow to spread. The subject was still given only a sketchy and naïve treatment in the textbooks that Peter read in the 1950s.

One reason for this deficiency is that the study of income is so difficult. If you get an assured wage of £x in cash per week, you may not unreasonably say that your income is £x per week. But as soon as the facts get less plain – as they will in even a simple firm – the difficulties start to pile up. Both the concepts and the task of choosing the figures are beset with doubts. So you must approach this part of your course with limited hopes. You will find yourself faced with many alternative ways of viewing income; the accountant must again and again make arbitrary choices between different figures that all have some merit and some defects. You may well in the end conclude that the accountant's best efforts must be only a poor attempt to weigh the imponderable.

Why then do we struggle to find such an elusive quantity? We use it for many tasks – to show a firm's progress; whether further investment is justified; and how much tax is payable. More important, it is a guide to the owner's consumption. A reasonable man may decide to spend more or less than his income, but he knows that overspending now will lessen his future welfare, and underspending will raise it. So he needs a base-line that reveals the 'over' or 'under'.

That notion gets support from Sir John Hicks' much-quoted definition: a man's income is:

> The maximum value which he can consume during a week, and still expect to be as well off at the end of the week as he was at the beginning.
>
> Hicks (1939)

INCOME AS GROWTH IN WEALTH

(a) Flows and capital maintenance

The fun starts when we try to measure 'can consume' and 'well off'. A highly abstract approach looks to flows of satisfaction: 'psychic income' is a person's flow of utility from consumption. Accounting must needs content itself with something more down-to-earth. It equates 'well-offness' with capital (wealth) measured in money. And it then links income with 'that amount which can be consumed without encroaching on capital' (Adam Smith's words). Which means that we must use ideas of *capital maintenance,* and that to measure income we must first know how to measure capital.

This may seem somewhat at odds with the helpful analogy of the stream and lake – the view that income is a flow during a period, whereas capital is wealth at a given moment (such as the year-end). But there is in fact no contradiction. If not dissipated, the flow adds to wealth. So, with straightforward facts, we may say that income for a period is the difference (after allowing for the owner's drawings and in-payments) between opening and closing capitals.

(b) Whole firm versus separate assets

Now for the first source of confusion. When we approach the task of measuring wealth, we must be explicit about the contrast between measuring the whole firm as a composite unit, and measuring the separate assets one by one:

1. *Whole firm.* Here the firm is valued on a forward-looking (*ex ante*) basis – much as if it is to be sold – by discounting its expected future cash flows. (You will recall the rather similar DCF budgets used to find whether a new asset is worth buying.) The individual assets do not enter directly into the calculation.
2. *Asset by asset.* Here the accountant in effect looks around and draws up an inventory (his balance sheet) of all the separate assets and liabilities that he recognizes.

Clearly the figures in (1) for future flows must be highly subjective (indeed, often wild guesses); sometimes indeed they may be only vague impressions at the back of the mind. The figures in (2) often are relatively sober and clear; they emerge from the respected processes of book-keeping; and we find them friendly because they echo our childhood's notions of wealth. (We were told of the Sleeping Beauty's castles and fields and flocks and jewels, not her DCF expectations.) The paradox is that we use (1) – despite its uncertainties – for the really fundamental decisions (e.g. on the firm's price at a takeover, or whether to close down a branch), and (2) for lesser tasks (routine yearly accounts). Or, to put the matter in another way, the concepts in (1) satisfy an elegant logic, though the figures must be shaky; whereas the logic in (2) is crude, even if the figures are fairly sure and objective.

27

(c) *Ex ante* income

Routine accounts do not use (1). But perhaps we should in passing ask what balance sheets would look like if (1) were used.

Suppose that, at date 0, the owner of a firm expects it to yield a net cash flow of £1000 at the end of each year, and his capitalization (interest) rate is 10%; opening capital is thus £10000, as in column (i) of Table 2.1. If all goes as expected, the end balance sheet (date 1, column ii) will duly put income at £1000.

But suppose instead that the owner's outlook changes at date 1, and that his DCF value jumps to £12000. This could be because he now foresees future receipts of £1200 per annum. However, let us consider a more interesting possibility – that he still expects to get £1000 per annum, but his interest rate shifts to 8.3%; £1000 divided

Table 2.1 Opening and closing balance sheet – wealth measured *ex ante*.

	(i)	(ii)	(iii)	(iv)
Date	0		1	
		Expectations do not change	Expectations change	
			'Capital' not revised	'Capital' is revised
Cash		1000	1000	1000
DCF value	10000	10000	12000	12000
	10000	11000	13000	13000
Capital:				
original	10000	10000	10000	10000
gain				2000
				12000
Income		1000	3000	1000
	10000	11000	13000	13000

by 0.083 = £12000. He could now draft his balance sheet as in column (iii), raising income at a bound to £3000. Egged on by this lush figure, he might then – for example with the help of a £2000 loan – withdraw £3000 in cash for a consumption splurge. But mark the aftermath. That big withdrawal would reduce future net receipts (say, by interest on the loan) from £1000 to about 10/12 × £1000 = £833. Yet his capital would still be £833 divided by 0.083 = £10000. So this system of income measurement maintains a 'well-offness', not of future receipts, but of their capital value.

Hicks seems to have this interpretation in mind when he amplifies his words quoted earlier to re-define income as:

> The maximum amount which can be spent during a period if there is to be an expectation of maintaining intact the capital value of future receipts (in money terms).
>
> Hicks (1939, p. 174)

(d) Maintainable consumption level

But most of us would think accounts less than perfect if they told us to spend £3000 this year and only £833 thereafter. We should prefer a system that keeps this year's income at a maintainable £1000 per annum. We can do so by giving capital a £2000 boost (as in column (iv)) to £12000 – which, after all, is the figure that the owner would have used from the start if he had been a smarter prophet. The extra £2000 can be labelled 'capital gain', if we use that overworked phrase in the sense of capital revision.

To stress constant consumption rather than its present value, Hicks offers us an alternative to his earlier definitions. Income becomes:

> The maximum amount a man can spend this week, and still expect to maintain future spending at this week's level.
>
> Hicks (1939)

A third definition again stresses constant consumption, by allowing for change in the price level (as during inflation): 'future spending' must then be defined in *real terms.*

Forward-looking income calculations (like Table 2.1) are almost unknown to routine practice, and probably always must be. Yet the thinking behind them has influence. Hicks's words are, for instance, quoted as gospel by advocates of inflation accounting. And the notion of *maintainable income* – useful as a guide to both investment and consumption – has forced published reports to show a 'profit on ordinary activities' that omits capital gains and also 'extraordinary' items (not from ordinary activities, but abnormal in size) and 'exceptional items' (from ordinary activities). But the selection and measurement of these items must often involve arbitrary judgements.

WEALTH AS NET ASSETS

If we brush aside psychic flows and *ex ante* aspirations, we come to familiar ground. We link income with growth in the sum of the net assets, listed item by item.

(a) Balance sheet v. profit and loss account

The income figure appears in both balance sheet and profit and loss account. But we can choose which of the two calculations to deem senior. Do we put our main stress on comparison of:

1. Net assets at the start and end of year, or
2. Costs and revenues?

In principle, the two yield the same answer. But in fact each is apt to colour the thinking of its votaries – sometimes to the point of varying the answer. The framework that I shall later use depends on (1); in my view, (1) is generally simpler, clearer and less prone to fallacy. However, (2) is more fashionable. But I believe that it brings several dangers. Thus it may treat the balance sheet as a mere depository for awkward figures, with scant regard to their significance and values. Again, it can confuse the clerkly processes of book keeping with observations of actual events. Fine phrases such as 'distributing cost in a systematic and equitable manner', and 'matching costs with revenues', hint that transfer of symbols in the ledger is an adequate substitute for regard to economic fact. In the real world, I have yet to run into an expiring cost.

(b) When does an asset exist?

The approach via the balance sheet forces us to ask 'What constitutes an asset?', i.e. when does a possible item merit inclusion in the list?

Tangible things (such as machines and cash) may present few problems. Rights to future receipts, if quantifiable and backed by a legal contract, also seem worthy (e.g. debtors). But how about hopes of getting a dividend? Or research, or an advertising campaign, or brand names? These dubious candidates are the cause of much debate; many of the topics discussed later could be regarded as subheads of the inclusion problem. Unhappily, our item-by-item method seems to lack a logic that can solve the problem any better than would the tossing of a coin. We must often rely on custom rather than reason.

(c) Comparison over time: capital measurement units

If we are to compare wealth over time, then the measurement units are important. In other words, we should ask whether the £s used for valuing the opening capital have the same worth as the £s used for the closing assets. Ideally they should of course be the same, but inflation destroys the likeness. ('Opening capital' is shorthand for all items in the owners' equity, e.g. share premiums.)

The need for like units should be the starting point for any reform proposals. Failure to correct opening capital with the *general* index helps to explain why our profession's proposals for inflation accounting foundered so ignominiously.

We must consider three possibilities – money units, real wealth units, and physical units:

1. *Money units.* The usual accounting method is based on these. If the ledger puts January's capital at £1000 and December's net assets at £1100, then income is £100. But does this make sense if the year's inflation has cut the £'s value by, for example, 25% as in 1974?
2. *Real wealth units.* Where this is the basis, the January £s of capital are brought up to date for the December balance sheet, i.e. the starting figures are raised into units of current purchasing

31

power (CPP) with the general index. Thus like is compared with like. To my mind, there is an unassailable case for such clarity and caution if income is to be a serious guide.

3. *Physical units.* This sounds an improbable basis for ordinary accounting, but it is in fact used sometimes, in disguised forms. If opening stock is 100 tons valued at £1000, LIFO still values 100 tons of closing stock at £1000, and adds or subtracts £s only if there are extra tons or 'decrements'. The proposal to tackle inflation with 'current cost accounting' (CCA) relies on much the same trick. If your studies in economics have sunk in, you must feel that wealth is more a matter of satisfactions and market values than physical characteristics, and so you will look askance at such methods.

Having disposed of capital, we can now move on to other items in the balance sheet and ask when and how their growth should be measured, i.e. how they should be valued. There are quite a lot of ways, and so quite a lot of income figures are conceivable; if there are n ways, it follows that – as there are also the three possible capital units – there are $3n$ methods of measuring income.

(d) Recognition stages for changes in asset values

From the standpoint of a book-keeper, growth concepts hinge on the point in time at which he is prompted to update his asset balances to current level. But which point should he choose? Income does not in fact burst forth at one clear moment, like the hatching of a chick. Usually there is a long series of stages, during which the income grows ever more sure and measurable. For instance, the main stages may include:

1. Having glimpsed the far-off possibility of gain, the businessman starts to deploy his assets (e.g. by investing in securities or raw materials).
2. His assets mature in a demonstrable fashion (e.g. securities appreciate, raw materials become finished goods).
3. He becomes entitled to payment (perhaps postponed), say by performing services or selling goods.
4. He receives cash.

5. He at long last becomes sure that the receipt of cash cannot be nullified by, for example, allowances for bad work, return of faulty goods.

Each of these stages has some claim to be regarded as the point at which income arises. In an ideal world, an income statement would have a number of columns, each based on a different stage, and each putting profit into a different period. The rival figures would all contribute to the general picture.

In fact, each firm chooses only one of the stages, most often (3). But let us next touch on other possibilities.

GROWTH IN CURRENT VALUE RECOGNIZED

Suppose first that a daring book-keeper puts in new figures as soon as value changes, i.e. at stage (2) of our list.

In deference to my liking for income measurement via balance sheets, let us arrange these in a series of columns that reflect successive book-keeping steps. Forgive me if, to keep my mind clear, I take insultingly simple examples. Suppose first that a firm's transactions are:

Date (a)   It starts with £10 in cash.
Date (b)   It buys an investment for £10.
Date (c)   The investment appreciates to £13.
Date (d)   The investment is sold for £14.

Table 2.2 shows the whole history at a glance. A form of income (preferably qualified as 'unrealized') emerges already at date (c), when value rises.

(a) Alternative forms of current value

However, 'current value' turns out to be more complex than our Table 2.2 suggests (as the accounting profession found when it tried to update its figures during inflation). A valuer has four main possibilities:

1. *Entry value.* Often this is buying price, but 'replacement cost' is a better term. For instance, it justifies the use of a net value

Table 2.2 Successive balance sheets, income recognized at appreciation date (c).

Date:	(a)	(b)	(c)	(d)
Assets:				
Cash	10			14
Investment – at cost		10		
after appreciation			14	
Owner's wealth:				
Starting capital	10	10	10	10
Growth – unrealized			4	
– realized				4
	10	10	14	14

where a higher priced replacement brings lower running costs.

2. *Exit value.* That is sale, price – or, where sale brings charges for commission, delivery, etc., net realizable value (NRV). This has the merit of alerting owners to the possible advantages of selling off underexploited assets; and, where the firm will in fact sell the asset and not replace it, no other figure seems pertinent. For most firms, however, the sale of fixed assets is out of the question; indeed, when assets are essential links in a productive chain, sale of one would spell disaster. So sale price often has scant relevance. Moreover, where assets are designed specially for a particular firm, but do not suit firms with other methods, NRV may be absurdly low or even negative; its use would then entail initial write-downs of great size, which might indeed make the firm buy less efficient assets with higher scrap prices. So exit values have many faults.

3. *Use value* (or 'economic value'). This looks to the benefits – often cash flows – that the asset may yield. Thus, when a firm considers buying an extra machine, it may draft a DCF calculation to compare (3) with (1); it will buy if (3) exceeds (1). But routine revaluation of all assets on this basis would be laborious

and highly subjective, and the summing of their separate marginal benefits must tend to result in a meaninglessly high total for the whole team.

4. *Deprival value* (or 'value to the business'). This selects judiciously from (1), (2) and (3) according to the actual circumstances of the particular asset. It does so by asking how much poorer the owner would be if he no longer possessed the asset (e.g. if he uses up stores or wears out machines): its value is the difference between having it and not having it. Normally 'not having' would make him replace, and so replacement cost is by far the most usual answer. If, however, the asset is not worth replacing, the deprived owner would follow the more rewarding of two courses: he would either keep it in use or sell it; so its value is here the higher of use value or NRV.

In short, (4) seizes on the good qualities of (1), (2) and (3), but avoids their defects. It seems to me the right choice.

(b) Extent of CV's use in practice

Historical cost (HC) accounts involve less work than current value accounts, and are deemed to be more objective. So, despite the extra information given by up-to-date figures, the accounting profession has for the most part set its face sourly against them.

You may therefore suppose that CV has no relevance save in radical schemes of reform (e.g. inflation accounting). But, as you will see, it is in fact used where circumstances make HC difficult. Farm accounts come at once to mind. I shall return to them later.

HISTORICAL COST

As you know, most accounting is founded on historical cost. Value is frozen until stage (3) of the list on p. 32 is reached. If the transactions are as in Table 2.2 except that the sale is for credit, then HC balance sheets assume the familiar forms of Table 2.3.

Obviously the book keeper's job is kept simple and easy if he makes no change before stage (3). But then external transactions force activity on him. If for instance he does not record credit sales

Table 2.3 Successive balance sheets, income recognized at sale date (d).

Date:	(a)	(b)	(c)	(d)
Assets:				
Cash	10			14
Goods		10		
Debtor			14	
Owner's wealth:				
Starting capital	10	10	10	10
Profit			4	4
	10	10	14	14

in customers' accounts at date (c), the whole process of collecting cash may break down.

Though our respect for stage (3) grew originally from book-keeping convenience, HC has other merits. It is familiar. It is easy to understand. It recognizes the importance of increased liquidity (i.e. the asset's march towards more objective values and finally cash). Because its figures are somewhat more certain than current values, the auditor can tick them happily, and they leave less scope for dispute over the size of, for example, tax, dividends and commission on profit. And, when general prices are rising, HC gives a cosmetic flush to the income statement (which helps to explain the rejection of inflation accounting).

But the system is not free from faults. In particular:

1. The historical cost of an asset (column (b) in Table 2.3) may be debatable.
2. The moment for recognizing growth ('profit realization', i.e. progress from column (b) to (c)), may also be debatable.

We next consider these faults in turn.

DIFFICULTIES OF FINDING HC

(a) Sequence troubles

Suppose my transactions are:

Date 1: I buy an asset for £7.
Date 2: I buy an identical one for £13.
Date 3: I sell one for £30.

Here HC puts my profit at either $£(30-7) = £23$, or $£(30-13) = £17$, according to whether (actually or notionally) I happen to pick up assets by the FIFO or LIFO sequence. Yet an onlooker who does not suffer from the 'trained incapacity' of accountants might well put profit at £40:

	£
Closing assets:	
Cash	30
Asset, at current value	30
	60
Opening capital	20
Gain	40

He would argue that my closing wealth depends on what is actually there, not on such a triviality as past physical sequence. The HC system lacks any inherent logic with which to refute him. Accounts that contain HC stock values can be defended only for their convenience and caution.

(b) Ingredient troubles

A factory accountant can gather all the obvious costs, and – making brave assumptions – split them between products. In consequence, he can beget a 'cost' for each item of stock, and a 'profit' when it is sold.

Here again HC can be justified by its convenience. But a critic trained in the marginalist tradition of LSE will look askance at the slices of overhead charged to various products; he will argue further that the figures depend on choice of allocation base (direct labour costs or hours, machine hours, etc.), and that we have not – and never shall have – any convincing logic for showing which of the bases is 'right'.

(c) Current value used where cost is unknown

In some enterprises, HC is impossible to apply. Farms are an example. Both farms and factories produce and sell things. Yet their accounts must be very different, and it is worthwhile to ask why.

Farms and overhead
A farmer may not be a meticulous compiler of figures. And, even if he were attracted by the claims of cost accounting, probably he would soon have doubts about allocation. How should he split local taxes between a calf and its mother, and interest between bees and barley? How should he allow for the difference between winter and summer activity? Experts sometimes try to devise a system for him, but the trouble and absurdity usually cause even a hardened cost accountant to falter. Thus much of a farmer's stock cannot be valued at HC. He must use other figures – probably some form of current value (and part of his income then accords with Table 2.2).

Physical accretion
There is another contrast between farm and factory: animals breed and machines do not. So farm accounts will include calves etc. as well as their parents, i.e. recognize assets that have no purchase cost. Where asset numbers grow, there is a strong case for increasing the income figure; farm accounts would be a poor guide to the year's doings if they left out the births.

However, the argument can hardly stop at animals. When crops are ripening, the farmer's wealth is growing just as surely as when calves are born, so his income should allow for this appreciation too. The same reasoning can be applied to forestry, on which Hatfield (1927) makes a further point:

> The product is becoming yearly more valuable. The increased value, if unquestioned, is akin to the increasing value of a discounted note which by most authorities is counted as income

available for dividend even though it has not as yet been converted into cash. (p. 253)

On the other hand, notes and crops usually become cash in a matter of months, whereas trees take decades. So prudence should perhaps dictate a dividing line – admittedly arbitrary – between fast- and slow-maturing flora and fauna.

Other breaches with HC – plantations and mines
Some exotic plantations and mines also value their stock at NRV. Possibly they too would have trouble in finding cost. And their products may sell (indeed have already been sold before the accounts are drawn up) in assured markets at quoted prices; in former days at least, some governments would take any quantity of gold and silver at fixed prices.

HC AND THE REALIZATION RULE

Under HC, growth in value is at last recorded when the asset is realized (date (c), Table 2.3).

Observing such records of a multitude of transactions in a multitude of firms, theorists have offered us the *realization rule*: the book keeper should enter value growth at stage (3) in the list on p. 32, though not sooner, because the new figure is then vouched for by an external transaction, and the cycle from investment to liquidity is rounded off (Table 2.3).

(a) The nature of realization

'Realization' thus suggests four things:

1. Completion of an *external transaction,* i.e.
    (a) A contract with an outsider (e.g. for sale of goods).
    (b) An earning process (activity and expenditure that enable the firm to fulfil its side of the bargain).
2. Resulting *liquidity,* i.e.
    (a) Conversion into cash, or at least into 'near cash' assets (debtors, securities, etc.).
    (b) Easy and sure valuation of 'near cash' assets.

39

There are plenty of firms where transactions involve all these four 'legs' of the full rule, and accountants have come to accept it as part and parcel of HC. But the full rule is unworkable, or at least highly inconvenient, in some circumstances. Then accountants have few qualms about modifying it (i.e. ignoring one or more legs) or abandoning it. It is not a procrustean bed into which, with resolute stretching and snipping, we can fit all firms and transactions.

(b) The law and the realization rule

This picture gets some confirmation from company law. Thanks probably to the influence of standards and the Second EC Directive, has been the rule enshrined in the Companies Act:

> Only profits realized at the balance sheet date shall be included in the profit and loss account.
>
> Companies Act 1985, Sched. 4, para. 12(a).

That sounds forthright enough. But nearby words show that the rule is in fact very much the junior in a team of three:

1. True and fair
2. Prudent
3. Realized.

Moreover, a later paragraph further emasculates the rule, with a seeming volte-face that must surprise the non-lawyer; realized profits are such profits:

> as fall to be treated as realized profits . . . in accordance with principles generally accepted with respect to the determination for accounting purposes of realized profits.
>
> (Sched. 4, para. 91)

In cruder words, the rule is to be thrown aside where it offends 'true and fair', or prudence, or accounting ways.

We saw earlier how the accountant discards the rule when dealing with farms. Let us next look at some of the circumstances in which he uses a modified version, for example by chopping off one or more legs.

40

(c) The external transaction

Leg (a): Contract with an outsider

Sometimes the contract tends to be only notional. Every student learns how to change profits by allowing for *accrued* rents and interest. Such change makes for more useful profit figures. But are we not stretching words if we plead justification by the objective test of an external transaction?

Here the difficulty stems from our definition of assets. As we said earlier, an 'asset-by-asset' approach to wealth must in effect look for the assets at some date, and list them in an inventory. Thus one can imagine an estate steward of earlier days itemizing fields, flocks and other assets that were obvious and tangible. Later his more enlightened successors came to hold that, if the estate accounts ran for the year to (say) March, and a tenant was sure to pay a £12 annual rent at the end of the following June, a £9 asset had already emerged by March, despite lack of an external happening; and likewise a liability for expenses could exist ahead of cash payment. Thus was born what in recent years has come to be called the accrual system: at his year-end, the accountant looks around for overlapping contracts, and writes up his ledger *as if* they produced actual cash movements for (say) each month till his year-end. The resulting accounts give a fuller view, and are a useful check on the efficiency of 'stewards'.

But, when looking for accruals, where does one draw the line? Rent receivable – under a precise contract and from a solid tenant – can reasonably be added to the asset list. Similarly some impending payments are so certain that they can reasonably be added to the liabilities. But other overlaps may be less sure and less quantifiable. The accountant must in each case draw a very arbitrary line – with which others might warmly disagree – to separate the admissible from the inadmissible. Thus he tends to allow for expected receipts of interest but not of equity dividends, and to include expected payments more readily than expected receipts.

Leg (b): Earning

Looking at the list on p. 32, you might reasonably think of income as growing gradually over the five stages. But, as you know, the book-keeper records all the growth at one stage (as in Table 2.3).

Some theorists say that this entry marks a 'crucial event', presumably the culmination of the *earning* process.

In most firms, venerable practice leaves little doubt about the date of this entry (e.g. the delivery of goods to, or their earmarking for, a debtor). But, as tax cases show, there are circumstances in which lawyers can disagree about the earning date. Thus a firm of underwriters at Lloyds wrote risks in return for a percentage of profit. If risk was underwritten in Year 1, work had still to be done in Years 2 and 3 (e.g. re-insurance, payments of losses). Commission was not calculated or paid till the end of Year 3. The firm argued that, as there was 'nothing ascertainable, demandable, or payable' till Year 3, the profit was not made till then. But the House of Lords held that it was made in Year 1 (*CIR* v. *Gardner, Mountain and D'Abrumenil Ltd* (1947); 39 TC 537).

Again, consider the earning process where there are *long-term contracts*. If the firm agrees to manufacture 5000 widgets at the rate of 1000 a year, the delivery of a year's batch may not unreasonably be deemed a realization. But where the contract is not physically divisible into yearly slices (as with the building of a skyscraper), strict doctrine must put off realization till final completion. This might make the contractor's profit fluctuate wildly over the years. Accordingly most accountants are willing to soften the doctrine and – with cautious provisos about future risks – to write up an asset account (e.g. by the 'percentage of completion' method) as if separable units were in fact delivered. An architect's certificate may give some objectivity to measures of completion. 'True and fair' here overrides prudence.

But which of his asset accounts should the contractor plump up? Increase in the HC of work-in-progress would be too blatant a breach of the Companies Act. So the Accounting Standards Committee tells us, in its Jesuitical Exposure Draft 40, to re-baptize the increased asset as 'amounts recoverable under contracts', a kind of debtor. A rose by another name can smell a good deal sweeter.

The earnings leg justifies our treatment of *revenue received in advance* (for example, subscriptions to magazine publishers and premiums to insurance offices). Cash grows, but this revenue cannot yet be regarded as earned. So we include also an offsetting liability until the firm discharges its side of the bargain. There may, however, be arbitrary decisions over the size of the liability, for example the proportion of insurance premiums to be carried forward into next year.

(d) Liquidity

Here again, two legs are often present at realization but we do not treat them both as essential.

Leg (a): Conversion into cash
The stages on p. 32 led up to growth of cash. Without the cash – or at least 'near cash' assets that enable the firm to borrow from its bank – a profit figure might be a poor guide to possible out-payments and hence consumption; again, payments of tax could bring disaster if assessed profit bore no relation to means of payment – one of the objections to a wealth tax. (But of course a firm may, after realizing cash, reinvest it in fresh ventures, and so wipe out the liquidity. The income figure merely points to liquidity at some stage during the year. Its usefulness falls unless cash budgets are respected.)

Not every external transaction leads to liquidity. Early accounting textbooks gave instruction in barter, and perhaps today's writers are giving us weak generalizations by dealing only with cash flows in their theories. Payment in kind still persists. Consider for instance a well-known transaction of the 1930s. An oil company sent crude to Germany and refined it in a subsidiary there. The Third Reich lacked the foreign exchange needed for normal payment. The company instead took new tankers from German yards, and added them to its fleet (fixed assets). So here was realization (or something very like it) without liquidity. Should value gain from such deals be treated as unrealized? Prudence would seem to say yes, but 'true and fair' must surely argue no. Omission of the gain would cause the accounts to give a poor picture of the year's trading, and would belittle the subsidiary's operations; and, if the company has other sources of liquid assets, there would seem to be slender grounds for withholding dividend.

Leg (b): Easy and sure valuation
Liquid assets can normally be valued more readily than fixed assets. But a seemingly sure figure – especially for debtors – may in fact be undermined by risk of non-payment or by claims for defective work, etc. A cautious firm offsets such an asset with a provision, the size of which must often be a matter of personal outlook. In extreme cases, the firm may postpone growth recognition till cash reaches the till – the 'cash basis' of measurement.

(e) Risk and the cash basis

If you are not too weary, you will have noticed that so far I have not mentioned stage (4) in our list from p. 32.

Our textbooks should be more explicit about the effect of risk on methods of income measurement. Two firms may operate in much the same way, and yet feel impelled to use different methods because they perceive different degrees of risk, or react differently to the same degree. Thus, where debtors' payments are capricious, a firm may feel that sale contracts (even with bad debt provisions) are a poor proof of asset growth. The firm will then ignore growth till the cash comes in, i.e. use the cash basis of stage (4). Examples may be found in retail trades where customers pay by instalments.

Long delays and high interest rates are another reason for choosing stage (4). They make (3) unsuitable unless discount is deducted from remote debts (and gradually written back over the years to maturity). High 'after-costs' of collection also argue for (4).

In many professional firms, risk can hardly be important. Yet some of them (even prestigious legal and accounting giants) reputedly cling to the cash basis. Their reason may be not unconnected with tax. And they may wish to show what can safely and conveniently be paid out to partners each year or at retirement.

(f) Value decline without realization

A sound economic rule tends to be symmetrical (e.g. applies alike to supply and demand, to production and consumption). We might therefore expect the realization rule to apply to value *fall* as well as growth. It does not. Consider two obvious cases of inconsistency — of value reduction without realization.

Lower of cost and market
When the current values of stock items sink below their cost, our general practice is to write them down (on the 'pick and choose' basis). This asymmetry is defended on grounds of prudence.

Depreciation
In Victorian times, there was still a belief – particularly gratifying to tax officials – that depreciation ought not to be treated as a cost: it could be shrugged off as a 'capital loss'. This may not have mattered where assets had short lives, so that costs of renewals could be charged against profits. But it did matter with long-lived assets such as buildings and mines. Critics have blamed failure to charge depreciation, and the consequent lack of replacement funds, for the dilapidated state into which many British factories fell and the failure has enabled South African gold mines to show higher profits and thus mislead investors. Now there is a general belief that all assets with finite lives should be depreciated.

But an industry with enough political clout seems able to bend principles. Our property lobby – displeased at the thought of lower profits – has wrung a dispensation from the Accounting Standards Committee. 'Investment properties' need not be depreciated, but are to be shown in the balance sheet at their open market value; value changes are to be kept in an 'investment revaluation' account (though a deficit on that account is to be charged against profit).

This breach of the rule seems sadly inconsistent with both the 'true and fair' and prudence criteria, and may bring much odium on accounting at the next slump in the property market.

CONCLUSION

Scientists hold that, if a principle is sound, it will repeatedly yield consistent results when different persons apply it in different circumstances.

It would be gratifying, and good for public relations, if accounting had an 'income principle' of which the same could be said. But accountants have to measure something that differs from the subject matter of science. The wealth of a firm – let alone the well-offness of its owners – has many facets, and we are surely not unreasonable if we in each case judge which facet best suits the given firm's nature and risks. This means that we must retain some variety of methods, and be ready in each case to justify an income figure that may have respectable rivals.

To be sure, laws and standards have to some degree narrowed the variety, and no doubt this process will go on. But we may well doubt whether the wisdom of future standards committees, or the brilliance of future researchers, can ever give us a principle that does away with variety and arbitrary judgement. You may ascribe this failure to the limitations of our (necessary) asset-by-asset structure and (perhaps unnecessary) HC values, and in part you will be right. But a shrewder explanation must also cite something still more fundamental: 'well-offness' is an elusive and many-sided notion that varies from person to person and from moment to moment. Let me quote Hicks (1939) once more:

> We may now allow a doubt to escape us whether it does, in the last resort, stand up to analysis at all, whether we have not been chasing a Will-o'-the-Wisp.

(p. 176)

REFERENCES

Hatfield, H.R. (1927) *Accounting: Its Principles and Problems*, Appleton, New York.
Hicks, J.R. (1939) *Value and Capital*, OUP, Oxford.
Smith, A. (1776) *The Wealth of Nations*, London.

3

A decision required on decision-orientated accounting

MICHAEL BROMWICH

This brief article reviews, in an informal way, the impact on financial (external) accounting practice of those accounting theories which seek accounting information that should help the users of accounting reports in their decision-making, especially their investment decisions. An alternative view of accounting is then presented which provides an explanation for many current practices in financial accounting, explanations for which have been found to be problematic when accounting is viewed from a decision-making perspective. Finally, some of the implications of this suggested view of accounting for policy-makers and for those who wish accounting to aid decision-making are considered.

It is now well accepted that since the late 1960s external (financial) accounting theory has undergone a revolution, at least in the academic literature and in the minds of a number of accounting policy-makers. In essence, and put crudely, this revolution amounts to a substantial move away from stewardship accounting towards seeking to meet the perceived needs of the users of accounting reports (see Beaver (1981), Chapter 1).

The process that has led to this change has been variously described and the chronology of the various theoretical approaches contributing to this alteration in emphasis has been variously classi-

47

fied. One very helpful description of the possible process is AAA (1977), Chapter 2. The agreed general direction of this change in the theoretical approaches to accounting was first a move away from codifying 'best' practice through searches for an 'ideal' accounting system, to considering the accounting needs of those using a variety of normative decision models. The most recent developments in this process are the incorporation of elements of information economics (Beaver (1981), Chapter 1) and agency theory (see, for example, Watts and Zimmerman (1978)) into decision-orientated accounting models, both of which have some-what reduced the normative content of these endeavours. This deci-sion-making orientation has affected the views of at least some accounting policy-makers. This approach has become central to the Financial Accounting Standards Board's Conceptual Framework Project. This is amply illustrated by the FASB's Statement of Finan-cial Accounting Concepts Number 1 (FASB, 1978) which says that 'financial reporting should provide information to help present and potential investors and creditors and other users in assessing the amounts, timing and uncertainty of prospective cash receipts' (para-graph 37).

However, a number of commentators have argued compellingly that it is difficult to discern any really concrete effects of this decision-orientated approach on the extant form of external accounting statements. Hakansson (1978), for example, when commenting on recent contributions of what here is called the decision-orientated school says:

> . . . More recent writing most certainly appears to have had a negligible impact [on practice] with the possible exception of statistical sampling techniques in the area of audit planning and work in replacement cost accounting on the SEC disclosure requirements in that area. This is, at least, indirect evidence that, despite a high level of activity, the normative research of the last 35 years and our recently initiated formal-ization of empirical research, have not led to any major advances in accounting knowledge.
>
> (p. 721)

Henderson and Peirson (1977), after reviewing the development of accounting theory, came to similar conclusions (pp. 137–42). Fully substantiating these views is a difficult, if not impossible, empirical task, but armchair empiricism does provide some informal confirmation. Inspecting present day accounting statements suggests these are still very much based on conventional, generally accepted, accounting principles with their emphasis on prudence and objectivity. Notwithstanding the above statement of the FASB, the outputs of standard setters and other accounting policy-makers can be claimed to be still firmly grounded in conventional practice. Only a few accounting standards world-wide show any real sign of being explicitly affected by the decision-orientated approach to accounting. These have been among the most controversial of standards – price change accounting and leasing provide illustrations of this controversy.

It is far easier to cite examples where standard setters have deliberately chosen conservative, rather than decision-orientated, treatments for accounting problems. The mandatory writing off of research and development in the period in which the costs were incurred provides an example. The confirmation by a large number of standard setting bodies of the conventional practice of including fixed overheads in inventory, or stock, valuation in the face of almost unanimous opposition from academic writers, is another. This view of financial accounting seems to have almost exact parallels in management (internal) accounting. For instance, the academic and educational literature is full of compelling arguments against using overhead allocation in decision-making which have had little or no impact on practice.

In contrast empirical work based on the decision-orientated view of accounting has been used by financial accounting policy-makers, mainly in an adversarial way. Empirical research, favouring a given viewpoint on an accounting problem, has been cited by those supporting this approach. Other empirical work has been quoted favourably by those seeking an alternative treatment (see Watts and Zimmerman (1979) for a rationale of this phenomenon).

The empirical work from the decision-making school, where this has been concerned with investors, has suggested the information provided in accounting reports presently yields little aid to those decision-makers who are the central concern of FASB in its

Conceptual Framework Project. Crudely put, the evidence suggests that only some 10–15% of security price movements can be explained by the information contained in accounting reports (see, for example, Beaver (1981), Chapter 5). This, and similar empirical evidence, combined with the perceived minor impact on accounting practice, briefly reviewed above, indicates that the dominance given to decision-orientated accounting, at least in the research literature, should be reconsidered. Other models of thought might, therefore, be given renewed consideration. (See Butterworth *et al.* (1982) for examples of possible alternative approaches which are concerned with the utility of accounting for a variety of purposes only indirectly aiding decision-making.) The concern of Ijiri (1967) with performance monitoring and accountability gives an example of such an important alternative school of thought concerning the purposes of accounting. The remainder of this article suggests that accounting in practice may serve at least one additional purpose not generally considered in the literature and which is rather removed from decision-making and usefulness as usually defined. Such alternative possibilities may provide an explanation for a number of existing accounting phenomena which are difficult to account for from a decision-orientated or usefulness stance. It also considers briefly the implications of this view for academic endeavours and for accounting policy-makers.

CONVENTIONAL ACCOUNTING AS A 'SCORING' DEVICE

It will be argued here that conventional accounting reports may be seen to function as scoring devices. With this view, accounting reports compiled generally on historical cost principles may be regarded as reporting the formal and definitive result of the entity's financial activities during a period. In any process which continues over a long period of time there is often a natural tendency not to wait until the process terminates in order to evaluate it. Rather the question arises of how well we have done during some sub-period. The results ascribed to a sub-period will necessarily be artificial for any complex process involving interdependencies over time, but such results seem required for a variety of purposes. Even abstracting from interdependencies over time, any scoring system which attempts to summarize in a simple way the performance of a complex entity will be imperfect.

Such difficulties seem not to militate against the use of very arbitrary scoring systems in a wide range of human activities. Casual observation of games, for example, suggests that for scoring systems to be of use it is unnecessary that they make complete sense. Rather, it seems sufficient that the scoring function is understood and accepted by both players and spectators – enterprise managers and accounting report users in the accounting setting. Disagreement is more likely the less concrete is the outcome of the game. Less debate is, perhaps, possible about who 'won' an athletics race than about the winner of an ice skating competition or, more extreme still, a modern poetry competition. In the first case there will be general agreement that the winner is whoever first crosses the finishing line, subject to the constraint that no clear cheating was detected by the judges. In a closely fought race there may still be disagreement as to who fulfilled this condition, though use of technology can usually resolve such disagreement. Remaining disagreements will centre around whether one or more participants cheated. For many purposes, an imperfect system for detecting such cheating will be accepted by most people even though some rulings may well be thought incorrect. Even where the physical test of success is clear, there may still be those who feel that their favourite would have won if conditions had been different.

The judges become more important where clear physical tests of success are either not easily available or are not easy to understand. Their perceived neutrality between the players and their believed independence becomes important as does their lack of bias and their recognized competence as judges. Some would argue that these are qualities which auditors bring to their task and that until the financial results of an entity are certified or validated by these particular judges, its results do not amount to an official score (Ng, 1978). With this reasoning it is quite possible that audited financial statements will be valued even though they contain no new signals concerning events (Shaw, 1980, Chapter 5). They may, for example, confirm the degree of belief or validity attached to existing signals.

It could be argued that a complicated scoring system will not be abandoned with ease once it has been accepted and its likely results have been comprehended. The amount of publicity and discussion attached to proposals to change the rules of any fairly complex game and, therefore, to a change in the scoring system, supports this view. Similar arguments may provide one reason why many people seem unwilling to abandon historical cost and the accounting principles usually associated with it.

PROBLEMATIC ISSUES EXPLAINED

This view of conventional accounting may help to explain a number of phenomena which are not easily accounted for by the more popular decision-making approaches to accounting. This perspective may help us understand the supposed lack of impact on practice of these decision-orientated models of accounting (Mautz, 1975, and Hakansson, 1978). For example, the finding that conventional accounting has only a modest effect on security values becomes, perhaps, more comprehensible with the scoring view. The score reported by the enterprise may be thought to be only a vague guide to its future prospects in the same way that the result from one football game taken on its own may say little about a team's likely future prospects. Rather, the accounting score for a past period serves, as it were, to close officially the period's activities. The formal score for a period may be used for a number of legal purposes, for instance as a numerical basis for commencing taxation calculations. Such scoring systems must perforce be imperfect and any messages for decision-making which they convey may be difficult to determine. This view is supported by the present lack of either theoretical or empirical evidence which bears on how useful are the messages or signals actually obtained from accounting information for decision-making purposes. In any case, such signals are likely to be weak unless the circumstances encountered in the future are similar to those experienced in the period under consideration. That our team wins against weak opponents in ideal circumstances for our favourites may say little about its prospects against strong opponents in less favourable circumstances. A message may begin to form if our team continues to win against a wide range of opponents in a variety of different settings. This may help to explain why some financial analysts attach substantial importance to long runs of accounting results over a number of years. Ijiri (1967, pp. 43–4), in the context of account-ability measurement, goes so far as to say that accounting scores may serve not as surrogates or proxies for other measures, but may be accepted as measures of performance in their own right.

Under the scoring view of accounting we would expect only generally modest movements in security prices when financial results are announced which reflect a score different from that expected. Such movements are likely to be small if the argument is accepted that one score in isolation is unlikely to contain much information about the future which is not already yielded by other signals appearing during the financial period. Indeed, it is the essence of the scoring view of accounting that one might expect the impact of the signals from scoring systems to be small relative to messages from other sources, simply because of the lack of corre-lation expected between the scores of different periods. Signals from accounting scoring systems may often be in conflict with the infor-mation provided by other systems – the 'we were robbed' syndrome well known in sport. These latter signals may be given the greater credibility.

This view of accounting reports as scoring systems allows some explanation of the attachment of the practical world to capital maintenance concepts. These models are used to determine when a profit has been made by the enterprise. Thus, the historical cost accounting system declares a profit only after ensuring that the net revenues of a period after meeting all charges is sufficient to ensure that the historical amount of equity investment (subscribed capital) has been maintained. Advocates of stringent replacement cost accounting would argue for a different capital maintenance concept. They would declare a profit only if the physical capital of the entity has been maintained.

Such concepts of capital maintenance are not obviously consis-tent with decision-orientated models of accounting. Indeed, they seem to have no place in such models. With these future-orientated models the decision-maker's objective should be to do the best that can be done irrespective of whether capital is maintained unless capital is defined consistently with the decision-making model in mind. This is not the usual case with accounting capital maintenance. Capital defined in these terms forms no part of decisions but rather its maintenance is determined by the results flowing from decisions.

If a scoring view of accounting is taken, capital maintenance concepts play a clearer role, a positive score being announced for the period if capital has been maintained, using whatever concept of capital maintenance is favoured. The handicapping of the participants in a horse or a yacht race might be seen as a similar endeavour. Although such handicaps are based to an extent on past results achieved, they would seem essentially arbitrary. Their use seems to depend solely on their acceptability as does any utility deriving from capital maintenance concepts in the accounting world.

This scoring view of accounting may also help us to understand why many preparers of accounts (and, indeed, many users) seem very attached to existing valuation methods and existing formats for presenting accounting information. Time and time again proposals to alter accounting (by standard setters, for example) have been resisted by preparers mainly because of alleged adverse effects of these changes on reported profits or on security prices. Such attitudes may seem irrational to advocates of the decision-making view of accounting because there is evidence that the market can see through accounting figures to the underlying 'economic reality'. The empirical evidence suggests that accounting figures at best have only a minor effect on security prices. Thus, resistance to changes in accounting treatments cannot be easily based on the supposed effects of such changes on security prices. Other arguments can, of course, be mounted against changes in accounting treatments such as that any benefits of the changes are likely to be outweighed by their costs and any adverse economic consequences. These arguments are, however, usually made as a codicil to the argument that changes in accounting procedures will cause alterations in security prices via any changes in profits or net worth induced by the alterations in accounting procedures.

This reluctance to agree to changes in accounting treatments is rendered more comprehensible with the scoring view. Changing an existing accounting scoring system might be seen as overthrowing a system, achieving the acceptance of which may have been very time consuming and very expensive. Scoring systems, including accounting systems, may be seen as generally imperfect and possessing some aspects which are often difficult to defend other than by arguing that the system incorporating them is accepted by the relevant community. Altering any one element of such systems may provide an opening which allows the logic of other items to be questioned by those who are unhappy with the existing system, but who presently lack the power to alter the status quo when this is otherwise unquestioned. It should also be recalled that accounting figures may still serve purposes which can affect many people even if they do not have major effects on security prices. Managerial bonuses and incentive schemes are often tied to the profits reported in an enterprise's final accounts even though their results, in terms of rewards and penalties, may be at variance with actual conduct.

Scoring views also, of course, give tautological support to accrual accounting and to the ideas of fixed overhead allocations. Such procedures are difficult to defend from a decision-making point of view (see Beaver and Demski (1979), pp. 43–5, Baxter and Oxenfeldt (1961) and Zimmerman (1979) for some attempts to explain one or both of these procedures). With the view being espoused here, such procedures are necessary to produce a score. The logic of the procedures adopted does not necessarily matter too much as long as the methodology used is acceptable to the parties involved. This view would be refuted if compelling evidence was produced that accruals and allocations were useful in decision-making (see Beaver and Demski (1979), pp. 43–5).

THE EVIDENCE

This view of accounting as a scoring device would be refuted if the routine comparisons between the score of this period and that of the previous period, or recent periods, could be found to have any substantial correlation with changes in security prices, that is, if rational expectations models built on accounting scores provided predictions of economic interest. Crude comparisons of this type are usually published either by the entity itself or by analysts and financial commentators at the time the accounts are published. They seem to have little effect on security prices, presumably because investors and the market generally adjust these crude comparisons for the environment believed to have been faced by the enterprise during these periods. The above reasoning does, however, suggest that forecasts based on a longer run of financial results, including the current period's results, might have some effect on security prices. Those who have applied forecasting methods taken from the rational expectations literature to accounting data have found some evidence of this relationship (see Beaver (1981) and Foster (1986)).

Similarly, the scoring view of accounting could be refuted if major changes in accounting methods which were permissible within the existing rules for compiling accounting reports lead to a change in the prices of the securities of enterprises undertaking such changes. The empirical evidence is generally that the market 'sees through' such changes. Archibald (1972), for example, examined security price behaviour when firms changed their method of depreciation from the accelerated variant (useful for tax reduction) to the straight line method. This may increase reported earnings. He found no favourable effect on security prices. (For more on this see Foster (1986).) Such results have so far been seen in the literature as confirming that the market is concerned only with the underlying matters which are expected to affect an enterprise's future cash flows and as demonstrating that the market is not fooled by results obtained purely by accounting techniques which may put a 'gloss' on these fundamental factors (Beaver (1981) pp. 125–27). These results could be equally argued to provide support for the view of accounting suggested in this article. The hypothesis that accounting reports represent official scoring documents would also be refuted if it were found that alterations in the size of components contributing to this score, such as fixed overhead allocations in inventories (stocks), depreciation and the amount of period costs written off, affected security prices. There is little, if any, evidence that they do. Finally, and more important, there is no evidence that the introduction of variants of price change accounting as supplementary to the conventional accounting reports in a number of countries have had any real effect on security prices. (See Beaver and Landsman (1983) for some North American evidence, and Carsberg and Page (1984) for some United Kingdom evidence.) Thus, it can be argued that these additional procedures, which may be regarded as attempts to change the scoring system used for businesses, have little effect on security prices. This is what we would generally expect. Alterations in scoring systems that do not affect the real factors influencing competitive success will not change the skill rankings accorded to the players. We would expect any changes that are not neutral between participants to affect skill rankings – consider a change that ruled out the use of some types of vehicle in Grand Prix racing. Of course, supplementary accounting statements may be regarded as tentative and not amounting to true changes in the scoring function, a role seen here as being presently served by conventional accounting statements.

CONCLUSIONS

There is a cost to accepting the scoring view of accounting which is that accounting figures cannot be regarded as directly relevant to decision-making. The interpretation of an official score for the previous period is a matter for the individual user of accounting reports. This is equally true of other scoring systems. A clear win in a race by our favourite may be regarded as signalling the possibility of a good future performance, but this depends on the future competition. The future significance of a given score becomes more obscure as the game under consideration becomes more complex. Thus, as has been said, for this reason we would expect no clear correlation between a company's past financial results and its security values.

With this view, many of the empirical studies which use some sort of decision-making model to explore the effect of accounting information on security prices may be thought of as wrongly directed. The purpose argued here for financial reports is to give a clear score to the enterprise's past activities and not necessarily to help directly in decision-making.

It is not being suggested that decision-orientated empirical work should cease. Rather it is being argued that the scoring view of accounting, if accepted, would require additional empirical work designed to help the understanding of extant accounting phenomena and institutions and to aid in explaining their existence. Researchers should seek not only to criticize but also to understand the reasons for the existence of those items of accounting practice which they view critically. Unless accounting has evolved in a purposeless, random way even those accounting items which seem to serve no purpose today may well have had reasons for existence in the past. A demonstrable understanding by researchers of the reasons for the existence of accounting concepts may be a necessary first step in the modification or removal of redundant items.

This view of accounting casts a new light on the objectives which accounting standard setters and accounting policy-makers can be expected to seek. It places added weight on the need for acceptance by the major elements of the business community and suggests that the acceptance of new accounting policies cannot be left to demonstrating the ineluctable logic behind their derivation from decision-making models. The accounting scoring system seems to consist of a large number of fairly arbitrary components. The acceptability of any suggested alterations to the accounting scoring system may be fairly random. Those components which are selected for criticism at any given time may be thought to be a matter of happenstance. The choice of any given accounting problem for review by standard setters may be influenced by a number of factors by no means all of which have anything to do with a wish to improve decision-making. The treatment of deferred tax might provide an example of a change to accounting which does little to improve decision-making. Some accounting components may become gradually seen as making little sense, in that they come to be seen as arbitrary and are then changed, but perhaps not for the better.

The role of standard setters and, indeed, academics who wish accounting to aid decision-making in this setting is, therefore, to seek every opportunity to ensure that any alteration to accounting standards moves the accounting system further towards becoming a useful decision-making system.

The decision-orientated standard setters should expect their suggestions motivated towards this objective often to be rejected because these suggestions may come into conflict with well-established and more favourably regarded aspects of the extant scoring system. All who have participated in accounting policy-making will have been made forcibly aware of the seeming conflict between relevance to user needs and the prudence principle. Those accounting policy-makers who wish to aid decision-making might seek to acquire sufficient patience to endure participation in debates concerning whether one or another accounting treatment for a given accounting item is 'better', where better is defined in some fairly nebulous way not generally related to relevance to decision-making.

REFERENCES

American Accounting Association (1977) *Statement on Accounting Theory and Theory Acceptance*, Report of Committee on Concepts and Standards for External Financial Reports, AAA, Sarasota, Florida.

Archibald, T.R. (1972) Stock market reaction to the depreciation switch-back, *The Accounting Review*, 47 : 1, 22–30.

Baxter, W.T. and Oxenfeldt, A.R. (1961) Costing and pricing: the cost accountant versus the economist, *Business Horizons*, 77–90.

Beaver, W.H. (1981) *Financial Reporting: An Accounting Revolution*, Prentice-Hall, Englewood Cliffs, New Jersey.

Beaver, W.G. and Demski, J. (1979) The nature of income measurement, *The Accounting Review*, 54 : 1, 38–46.

Beaver, W.H. and Landsman J. (1983) *The incremental information content of FAS33*, Financial Accounting Standards Board, Stamford, Connecticut.

Butterworth, J.E., Gibbins, M. and King, R.D. (1982) The structure of accounting theory: some basic conceptual and methodological issues, in *Research to Support Standard Setting in Financial Accounting – A Canadian Perspective*, S. Basu and J. Alex Milburn (eds), The Clarkson Gordon Foundation, Toronto.

Carsberg, B.C. and Page, M.J. (eds) (1984) *Current Cost Accounting: The Benefits and the Costs*, Prentice-Hall, Englewood Cliffs, New Jersey.

Financial Accounting Standards Board (1978) *Objectives of Financial Reporting by Business Enterprises*, Statement of Financial Accounting Concepts No. 1, FASB, Stamford, Connecticut.

Foster, G. (1986) *Financial Statement Analysis*, 2nd edn, Prentice-Hall, Englewood Cliffs, New Jersey.

Hakansson, N.H. (1978) Where we are in accounting: a review of 'Statement on Accounting Theory and Theory Acceptance', *The Accounting Review*, 53 : 3, 717–25.

Henderson, S. and Peirson, G. (1977) *An Introduction to Financial Accounting Theory*, Longman Cheshire, Sydney.

Ijiri, Y. (1967) *The Foundations of Accounting Measurement*, Prentice-Hall, Englewood Cliffs, New Jersey.

Mautz, R.K. (1975) Some thoughts on applied research, in *Accounting Research Convocation: Bridging the Gap*, Previts G.J. (ed.), University of Alabama, Alabama.

Ng, D.S. (1978) An information economics analysis of financial reporting and external auditing, *The Accounting Review*, 53 : 4, 910–20.

Shaw, J.C. (1980) *The Audit Report: What It Says and What It Means*, Gee & Co (for the Institute of Chartered Accountants of Scotland), London.

Watts, R.L. and Zimmerman, J.L. (1978) Towards a positive theory of the determination of accounting standards, *The Accounting Review*, 53 : 1, 112–34.

Watts, R.L. and Zimmerman, J.L. (1979) The demand for and supply of accounting theories: the market for excuses, *The Accounting Review*, 54 : 2, 273–305.

Zimmerman, J.L. (1979) The costs and benefits of cost allocations, *The Accounting Review*, 54 : 3, 504–21.

4

True substance and fair reporting

HAROLD C. EDEY

In April 1986 I had some correspondence with Peter Bird in connection with a study he was conducting into 'front profit loading' in lease accounting. He commented that application of the maxim 'substance over form' calls for recognition of a 'normal form' which a given substance should take. This must surely be right. Form is the essence of accounting. Without form its function of digesting and summarizing what would otherwise be a mass of intractable material is lost. Indeed, one might paraphrase Peter's words in the aphorism, 'to each substance its appropriate form'.

The practising accountant has to decide what this appropriate form is in a particular instance. The reflections that follow bear on this question. The issues are hardly new but they are, I think, sufficiently fundamental to justify giving them another jaunt. They are certainly not yet widely appreciated.

DISTRIBUTABILITY AND PERFORMANCE

Many current problems arise from the fact that 'distributability' and 'performance' are both regarded as primary characteristics of the numbers generated by financial reporting. Reporting performance implies, I assume, an attempt to provide a picture which, when 'decoded' (to use one of Peter's terms), has commercial significance. But the higher such significance, the greater will tend to be the ratio of economic estimate to objective fact, and so the less appropriate for the legal function of deciding what can be distributed. So there is a trade-off.

One can easily forget how much the conventions of accrual accounting, when it grew up in the nineteenth century, were influenced by the need to determine what could be distributed by a limited company without breach of the law. A study of the 1928 edition of Dicksee's *Auditing* (the last edited by Dicksee himself) shows the importance placed by this influential early writer on the general tenor of the judicial decisions relating to distributability, even though he clearly distinguished between what should be regarded as accounting profit and what might be distributable in a specific case.

Dicksee identified what he called 'the true net profit earned' with the balance determined by application of the prudent conventional procedures. It is evident that he did not regard the 'prudent' approach as inimical to good performance reporting to shareholders, and that he considered that accounts prepared using this approach would, in his own words, 'enable them from time to time to judge of the value of their investment' (p. 300). This statement is the more noteworthy in that he was emphasizing the importance of providing information about subsidiaries, and informing shareholders of situations analogous in some respects to those referred to in the recent Accounting Standards Committee's Exposure Draft 42, Accounting for Special Purpose Transactions – situations where the normal accepted form of accounts would not necessarily disclose the existence of significant interests or risks.

So Dicksee was able to associate what we should regard as sound, indeed advanced, ideas on what was due to shareholders in financial reporting with the view that this obligation could be met by prudent accounting, that is, accounting appropriate for deciding what dividend could (subject to cash availability) be safely paid.

It would probably be wrong to assume that Dicksee and his contemporaries were influenced only by the strong bias towards legal aspects of the subject in accounting practice and education at the time. As children of the Victorian era they would also have been imbued with the almost moral importance of avoiding erosion of capital. This thought, and the consequential policy conclusion for reporting, comes through clearly in Pixley's comment that the directors' object ought not to be to pay as high a dividend as possible, but to do exactly the opposite (see Kitchen and Parker (1980)).

PROFESSIONAL VIEWS IN THE 1930s AND LATER

In the early 1930s Dicksee's *Auditing* was still regarded as a basic authority, as I know from my own experience, though for examination use it had by then been replaced by the more concise student texts. Such texts tended to be liberally sprinkled with legal references and a general concern for prudence ran through them. Someone like myself who got his (or exceptionally her) accountancy training in the 1930s was left in no doubt about the relation between reported profit and distributable dividends. It was accepted, as recognized in Dicksee, that there were oddities in the law, such that for dividend purposes past losses could be ignored and depreciation was not always an essential charge. But in general one accepted that the balance shown on profit and loss account was what could be distributed. The accumulated totals of such balances were the 'free reserves' – free, that is, for distribution. Nor, it should be added, were accountancy examinees expected to suggest that profit balances drawn up as the texts advised might be an imperfect measure of commercial performance.

At the end of the 1960s the contents of financial statements were still largely a matter for the practitioner, subject to presentation and disclosure in accordance with the Companies Acts. Such restrictions as there were on free choice of accounting treatment arose in large degree from acceptance by the profession generally of the approach inherited from the nineteenth century, referred to above. The limitations, as economic statements, of accounts drawn up under the traditional conventions had been recognized by academics for many years, notably by Hatfield, Paton and Canning in the United States and later by R.S. Edwards, Coase and Baxter in Britain. The beginning of more general recognition that a problem existed dates, I suppose, from the early 1970s when the ASC was set up under its then name of the Accounting Standards Steering Committee. But an accountant visiting from Mars might still have been surprised by the continued emphasis put by many on the question of distributability, legal or otherwise, as a criterion of performance measurement. This can only be attributed, I think, to the influence of the body of doctrine inherited from the nineteenth and early twentieth centuries.

What, one may ask, has distributability to do with performance reporting? Performance measurement, one assumes, is concerned with showing, on the basis of some selected model, how much better or worse off in some commercial sense the enterprise is as the result of a year's operations, whereas financial theory puts the dividend decision into the investment-financing decision box. Practical experience tells us that in real life a management's distribution policy is likely to be based on a programme for steady dividend growth. The arithmetic for assessing what the dividend figure should be in a particular year is to be found, not in the annual accounts, but in the cash flow projections. For those who are interested in performance, the financial report is merely one source of data which may help them in making their own projections. For this purpose the individual components of the accounts are likely to be of more significance than totals or bottom-line figures. The reported profit may be a legal restraint, but this is seldom the case as dividends can be paid out of accumulated reserves. As I write, directors of a bank which has reported a substantial accounting loss are not hesitating to maintain the current level of dividend.

It would, of course, be possible to formulate instructions for calculating 'profit' so as to tie it to the long-run potential distribution. 'Profit' of a particular year, it might be said, should be regarded as the amount that could be distributed in that year consistently with the expectation of maintaining the same level in succeeding years (cf. Hicks (1946)). It is interesting to note that such a definition comes to mind when one reads of the efforts of a mid-nineteenth-century railway manager to find a suitable set of procedures for annual profit reporting. (See the reports by Huish and others reprinted in Edwards (1986).) Those who believe that reporting on distributability can be consistent with reporting on performance should perhaps come down in favour of such a formula. I suspect, however, that, even were this legally possible, there would be no great rush to follow this path, for it would imply leaving much more than at present to the judgement of the directors.

THE ROLE OF STANDARDS

A great fuss was made in the media about the change in the AEI stock valuation which followed the successful GEC takeover in 1967. This clamour, we are reminded, was a major factor in bringing about the introduction of mandatory standards in Britain (see, for example, Leach (1981) and Watts (1984)). It seemed to me then, as it does now, that the problem was to a large extent spurious and that the fuss was really evidence of a serious and widespread failure to appreciate the nature and limitations of accounting reports. It is a criticism of the accounting profession – and no doubt of accounting teachers, including myself – that it has not been made clearer to financial journalists and to the lay public what accounts can and cannot do.

It ought not to surprise accountants, at least, that two different boards of directors, each with its own policies, should put quite different realizable values on the long-term contracts of the same company. Such differences may, however, seem odd to those who do not realize that such valuations must involve subjective assessment and are by their nature a function of the policy and plans of the people in control, as well as of their opinions and temperaments. Change the management or the management strategy and you change the assessments. There can be no uniquely 'correct' result. But the public at large has been allowed to believe that a standard formula is always available to settle such amounts and give the result a commercial meaning. Failure to find and apply such a formula is attributed to the incompetence of the accounting profession.

Standards can be divided into two types – those that call for descriptions and explanations of treatments that are in some way significant or unusual, and those of the bench-mark type which specify the form in which a particular kind of transaction will normally be reported and which, therefore, perform a kind of 'dictionary' function. The combination of the two can meet Peter Bird's case for specifying the normal form for reporting a particular substance, and can draw attention to instances where some departure from the norm has been considered necessary. But it is certainly a bad mistake to believe – and worse to lead lay persons and the press to believe – that such standards can or should avoid the kind of variations in estimation and assumption which led to the major difference in treatment of stocks in the GEC–AEI case.

Nor, since it is clear that there can be no uniquely 'correct' way of reporting performance, does there seem a strong reason why in suitable cases there should not be more than one standard way of reporting a particular matter, provided the treatment adopted is reported clearly and distinctly, and adequate attention is given to explanation and, where needed, interpretation.

GOODWILL

The argument over goodwill reporting is a good illustration of the disadvantages of attempting to find and standardize a 'correct' solution to every accounting problem. The topic is hardly new. Dicksee, writing in 1892, was unable to make a firm recommendation on how goodwill should be treated, but what he had to say then still has a ring of good sense. He comments:

> . . . No one who thought of purchasing a business would be in the least influenced by the amount at which Goodwill was stated in the accounts; in short the amount is absolutely meaningless.

(p. 127)

He concluded that so far as goodwill is concerned it does not matter much what you do.

The arguments between those who want immediate write-off and those who want goodwill written off by instalments to profit and loss can be represented as a conflict between two schools of thought. The 'record it and then amortize it' people consider their treatment will give a better assessment of performance in the sense of return on earlier investment. The 'write it off at once' school say that such treatment will give a false idea of performance by debiting annually to profit a meaningless amount. The 'record it and amortize it' argument would perhaps have more force in a regime of full current value recording, where the current economic cost of all assets, and not merely of those just acquired, was taken into account. Even then there is still the difficulty that the economic value of goodwill is inseparable from that of the business as a whole so that it is impossible to determine, without an overall valuation of the enterprise, how much goodwill has deteriorated or improved at any given later time, i.e. whether the original goodwill has been kept in 'good repair'.

This might suggest that, if goodwill cannot be left in the balance sheet, the 'write it off at once' group have the better case, for they are accepting the limitations of the accounting process. But the argument is further complicated by the fact that the treatment chosen may affect what may be distributed. 'Distributability' raises its ugly head again.

THE BASIC PROBLEM

Goodwill may appear to be a special case. In fact, almost all attempts to produce accounts that 'really' reflect economic performance run into the same basic problem, namely that whatever model you may choose, the assessment of how well you have done this year requires, if it is to be realistic, an estimate of the business legacy you are passing on to the future. A satisfactory accounting representation of this legacy calls for a set of management budgets or projections, the most important of which is a cash flow projection. The assets, liabilities and provisions in our traditional statements are no more than highly stylized reflections of what the future may hold, which cannot help leaving out part of the economic picture as the management should see it.

THE LEGAL RESTRICTIONS

Any attempt to move towards better performance reporting has to take account of the restrictions imposed by the EC company law directives, now reflected in British company law. Study of the Second and Fourth Directives suggests strongly that the overriding rationale of the accounting rules is the limitation of distributions to profits calculated by the application of traditional historical cost methods. It is true that some of the restrictions can be set aside where their application is not compatible with the general obligation to show a 'true and fair view', which might seem to leave room for development. But this derogation is only available in 'exceptional cases' and must surely be interpreted in the sense of the general philosophy of the Directive.

So it seems that the only scope for a significant move in the direction of what some at least would regard as better performance reporting lies in the use of Article 33 of the Fourth Directive. This permits ('pending subsequent co-ordination in the Community') the use of current cost accounting, while maintaining the historical cost principle for distributions. In Britain at present some freedom also appears to be available in that paragraph 91 of the Fourth Schedule of the Companies Act 1985 leaves the decision on what constitutes 'realized profit' to the accounting profession. It seems unlikely, however, that significant deviations from established historical cost usage in this context would be held to be consistent with European or, indeed, British law.

CONCLUSIONS

The problems of financial reporting for performance seem to call for action at two levels. There is a continuing need for a kind of 'care and maintenance' approach to keep the accepted procedures of historical cost accounting in good repair and improve them within the limits permitted by law. Much of the work of the Accounting Standards Committee has been at this level. But, apart from the possible use of CCA, it is difficult to see how major changes are possible within the framework of the main accounting statements now required by European law. In earlier years, and especially before 1948, innovation in financial accounting was achieved by example. Consolidated accounts – strongly opposed at first by leading accountants and businessmen – are a classic case. In Britain the early examples of these were, of necessity, published as statements supplementary to the legal accounts. This path remains open. Even when legal barriers are absent there is much to be said for it. It allows an initial period of trial and error. The act of innovation itself generates thought and discussion, as the CCA example shows – we have not seen the last of this development. Experience teaches. The inevitable early differences of opinion and consequential compromises can be assessed and sorted out.

Two matters seem worthy of particular attention in the search for better forms and presentation. First, there is surely a case for paying more attention in the process of standard making to the best management accounting procedures, untrammelled as they are by legal restrictions and nineteenth-century financial accounting practice. Secondly, there is a strong case for providing users of accounting statements with more interpretation of the figures. Good accountants have always known that interpretation is of the essence of good management accounting presentation. This notion has not flowed through to financial reporting.

Perhaps the best immediate service to users – not least to the financial press – would be to convey to them, as simply and as clearly as possible, the following truths:

1. Accounting reports can provide no more than approximate – 'rough' is a better term – indications of the financial results and state of a business. Study of the accounts as a whole, and especially of the component elements of the various totals, may, in conjunction with such other information as is available about the business and its environment, help the reader who understands them to make better conjectures about its state and prospects than would otherwise be the case. But the numbers should not be seen as precision measurements.
2. Understanding of the reports calls for an appreciation of the conventions of measurement used.
3. The significance of the numbers depends in part on assumptions by management about policy and the future progress of the business.
4. The profit numbers of any particular company have usually no well-defined predictive quality and there is no promise that the results they show will continue in the future.

REFERENCES

Dicksee, L.R. (1892) *Auditing*, reprinted 1976, Arno, New York.
Dicksee, L.R. (1928) *Auditing*, Gee, London.
Edwards, J.R. (ed.) (1986) *Reporting Fixed Assets in Nineteenth Century Accounts*, Garland, New York.
Hicks, J.R. (1946) *Value and Capital*, OUP, Oxford.

Kitchen, J. and Parker, R.H. (1980) *Accounting Thought and Education,* Institute of Chartered Accountants in England and Wales, London.

Leach, R. (1981) The birth of British accounting standards, in *British Accounting Standards,* R. Leach and E. Stamp (eds), Woodhead-Faulkner, Cambridge.

Watts, T. (1984) British accounting standards and the EEC, in *External Financial Accounting,* B. Carsberg and S. Dev (eds), Prentice-Hall, London.

5

The future of self-regulation

DON HANSON

(Based on an address to the Institute of Chartered Accountants in England and Wales Summer Conference 1987)

No system of regulation can stand still for long. Disciplines are subject to constant change and regulation, by its nature, must evolve with the changing activities of those it seeks to regulate. The essential features of a self-regulatory system are that it must be responsive to change, be able to adapt quickly and be capable of anticipating future events.

Practising accountants often assume that self-regulation must be in the best interests of the profession and society at large. This is a myth. There is no merit in self-regulation of itself. It is only to be favoured if it works more effectively than the alternatives.

On the whole, our profession has a good record in responding to change. The many activities of our members prove that. But today, change is both more rapid and more dramatic than it ever has been in the past.

Perhaps The Institute of Chartered Accountants in England and Wales, like other organizational structures, is not responsive to the immediate market place and has become too ponderous. We are at an important juncture and we can continue to prevaricate or we can move forward in a bold, imaginative and comprehensive way. Taking the lead will allow us to grasp the opportunities available; a failure of leadership will mean that others will take the initiative and impose solutions on us.

In this paper I consider the strengths and weaknesses of the present system and recommend changes based on my analysis. Inevitably, I must touch on many of the profession's most sensitive issues.

Personally, I welcome the initial position taken by the government in the Department of Trade and Industry's outline proposals published in 1987. The government has suggested that the professional bodies provide more explicit assurances than at present on the co-ordination, monitoring and enforcement of professional standards.

Many of the issues involved have already been considered by the Institute. But much of our discussion has been muddled by piecemeal review of individual issues and by a failure to agree on a comprehensive framework for self-regulation of the profession.

I would like to suggest nine elements which are essential if we are to be able to claim success for our self-regulatory system. Our profession should:

1. Concentrate on public interest entities: listed, USM, OTC and third market companies, plus of course, companies within the financial services sector;
2. Have a single point of contact with the government and other regulatory bodies;
3. Direct its primary administrative responsibilities to the firms which service most of the public interest entities;
4. Harness the strengths of the existing bodies and avoid the imposition of an intermediate body;
5. Recognize the need for more supervision and be more directly involved in practice administration;
6. Be positive in accepting new responsibilities when change is obviously needed;
7. Accept the need to monitor and enforce professional standards;
8. Urgently address the future development of financial reporting;
9. Establish an appropriate role for government.

At the same time it is, in my view, essential also that we organize our Institute more on the lines of the Worsley proposals (Institute of

Chartered Accountants in England and Wales, 1985), in order to make it more relevant and responsive to our profession's interests.

Let me cover these nine elements in more detail.

UNIFORM STANDARDS FOR ALL COMPANIES

This debate has been going on for decades and it is about time it stopped. We are virtually alone in requiring all companies with limited liability to adhere to common reporting standards. This retards the development of more demanding standards for entities of wider public interest. Probably 99% of the problems over standards relate to 1% of companies. If we want to be effective, we will deal with that 1%.

In my judgement we should readdress this issue as a matter of urgency since we will not achieve better self-regulation until we have sorted it out. The government, frankly, has a choice. Our profession can offer a great deal if we separate small companies from public interest entities and concentrate on the latter. But it can offer little if the same standards have to be applied to all limited liability companies.

THE NEED FOR A UNIFIED PROFESSION

To be more responsive to rapidly changing circumstances, short lines of decision-making are essential. No discussion on self-regulation will get very far without reference to the fragmentation of the profession. We have worked together well on issues such as auditing, reporting and discipline but there are many areas of duplication and overlap which drain our energies and dilute our results. Again, the arguments have been voiced for decades; what is now needed is a catalyst to get things moving. Perhaps we need the government to provide it. The DTI's message could not have been more forthright when it stated:

> ... The Secretary of State might be able to discharge his responsibilities more effectively if the Department could talk to the professional bodies and representatives of audit 'consumers' collectively rather than on an individual basis. This is

one of the points the Department would like to pursue in further discussion with the profession.

(DTI, 1987)

The government is impatient and the government is right to be impatient. Any faltering now and succeeding generations will look with amazement at the delay in integrating our profession and sharpening our decision-making.

THE RELATIONSHIP BETWEEN THE ACCOUNTING BODIES AND THE FIRMS THEMSELVES

Historically, the accounting bodies have avoided most forms of direct supervision over firms. This has been a strength and a weakness. Whilst Institute services have been broadly based and sensitive to the needs of individual practitioners, it has ignored the growing realities of the profession. It is clear that the old ways cannot survive in the new environment. The impetus for change will come from the new regulatory environment. It is a change long overdue.

The Financial Services Act 1986 will radically change the traditional relationship between the Institutes and the practising firms. Emphasis will have to shift from individual members to the firms in which they practise. I welcome this change. It brings the profession and our Institute into closer touch with the real world.

The Office of Fair Trading's Report on Professional Services, published in August 1986, cautiously recommends that the DTI consider the '20 partner' rule in the Companies Act. Solicitors and chartered surveyors and many of our members wish to operate multi-disciplinary firms and we should be allowed to do so. Both the government and our profession must remove the barriers which restrict our ability to compete and serve our clients.

The development of multi-disciplinary firms is likely to make the accounting bodies less relevant than they are today: another reason why such bodies must re-direct their attention to firms. What can the Institute do for a firm other than examine its students and discipline its members? It must seek ways to help the firm survive and prosper in a competitive and complex environment.

THE MOST APPROPRIATE STRUCTURE FOR OUR PROFESSION

The government has decided that the present system, through the recognized bodies, is consistent with its general approach to self-regulation. Ultimate, directional power will be with the Secretary of State, to ensure that the directive is being met. Following the recommendation of staying with the present system, each of the existing individual professional accounting bodies will need to comply with the rules laid down by the Secretary of State. One requirement under his recommendation is that the various bodies improve and mould themselves to be responsive to environment changes.

The proposal, then, preserves the essential element of self-regulation.

EXPANSION OF THE SUPERVISORY ROLE OF THE ACCOUNTING BODIES

The first major issue to arise over supervision concerns the authorization of investment business but other demands may also be made on us. Since most firms of chartered accountants are conducting investment business as defined in the legislation, most firms will need to be authorized if they wish to continue offering their present range of services.

Quite rightly, our Council has decided to obtain the status of a recognized professional body which under the Financial Services Act can authorize its own members. The Institute will expect to authorize the arranging of investment deals and the provision of investment management and advice so long as this type of business is not the main part of the practice.

The Securities and Investments Board will require the Institute to monitor compliance with its Conduct of Business Rules. This will involve passive monitoring and also some active monitoring such as visits to firms.

Our status as a recognized professional body will no doubt lead to further requirements of this nature. The reorganization of administration of the Inland Revenue following the Keith proposals may place more responsibilities on our profession to act in this kind of supervisory role, giving credibility to documents and returns made to the Inland Revenue. We must guard against unreasonable demands, but nevertheless, we must also be prepared to respond positively and promptly.

THE NEW REPORTING RESPONSIBILITIES

Inevitably the authorities will seek to impose extra responsibilities on the profession. We are right to be cautious but we should not be stubborn. If what is proposed is reasonable in the light of the changed environment, and if we are able to provide it, we ought to respond positively. On the other hand, if we think the requirements are unreasonable, we must vigorously reject them and work towards a solution that is acceptable. Our record for change in this area is commendable. New roles have been defined for us under the Building Societies Act 1986 and the Banking Act 1987, with Auditing Guidelines already published or at an advanced stage of development. I am sure that by assuming significant new responsibilities under the Financial Services Act we are also demonstrating the ability of our profession to respond to changed needs.

Internal controls and fraud are areas where the profession is being asked to take further responsibility and new demands will be made. Litigants are already assuming more responsibility than auditors thought they had.

We need to be responsive. We need to ask questions such as 'Do we have a role?' 'Is the role a professional role?' 'Does it allow us to employ our independence, objectivity and integrity?' If the answers are yes, then we should be willing to take on the new responsibilities providing the risk is manageable.

THE MONITORING OF AUDITING STANDARDS

The ability to monitor change and enforce standards is perhaps the single most important requirement of any self-regulatory body. In this regard, I believe that the accounting bodies' monitoring of the professional standards of their members has not matched the growing expectations of society. The time is right for a more effective means of monitoring the profession's performance and competence. An improvement in this area would benefit both the profession and society.

The government has underlined the importance of efficient monitoring. It has identified specific rules that the accounting bodies must be able to enforce. These are rules on the application of technical standards, on procedures for maintaining professional competence and on dealing with complaints and disciplinary sanctions.

The profession has come a long way in recent years in its efforts to improve performance. New techniques of auditing have helped to codify existing practices and to identify further necessary improvements. It is now a professional requirement that individual auditors refer to non-compliance with accounting standards, if non-compliance is not disclosed by the company. Auditors are required to state that they themselves have observed the relevant auditing standards.

Some of the professional bodies have set up a Joint Disciplinary Scheme. Although commendable, it has, in its efforts to be fair, been ponderous and slow. We need a system which is more practice-orientated and timely.

This is not an easy problem, since if we are in a position to deprive members of their livelihood, the laws of natural justice must apply.

We need some form of current review to help identify weaknesses before they cause trouble. I would like to see a system where licences for auditing public interest entities would be granted and withdrawn from individual firms. Here we would be looking at firms as a whole, assessing them regularly against a number of criteria. We would have to examine their quality control procedures; how they communicate these to their staff; the quality of their manuals on accounting, auditing, reporting and ethics: their independence, recruitment, training, personal assessment, promotion and discipline. We would have to look at the way they handled problem jobs, how they handled the people on those jobs and the litigation experience. The proposal is similar to the English Institute's concept of a training office with vetting procedures that need to be followed before a firm is recognized.

These reviews would be performed by employees of the recognized bodies supported possibly by secondees from individual firms. This is a difficult area since it does involve a creation of a separate bureaucracy and special thought will be needed as to how to keep this group dynamic and on its toes. Perhaps even a separately funded independent outside body could have this role.

In this area of monitoring and enforcing professional standards, I believe that there is a strong case for introducing minimum requirements for CPE that should apply to all members' reserved functions. As an experiment we should continue to allow members to monitor their own CPE but require them to report details annually.

THE FUTURE DEVELOPMENT OF FINANCIAL REPORTING

No assessment of the strengths and weaknesses of the present system would be complete without reviewing the achievements of the Auditing Practices Committee and the Accounting Standards Committee.

The APC has served the profession well. In the early years it concentrated on the codification of best practice – and in doing so it undoubtedly helped to raise auditing standards. More recently it has moved to more contentious issues and has showed an ability to address emerging problems with energy and speed and to move the profession forward on sensitive issues. I would observe, however, that the APC's distinction between auditing standards and guidelines is artificial. Many of these guidelines should become mandatory standards.

In contrast, the Accounting Standards Committee has been much less satisfactory. In its early years it was reasonably good at addressing and resolving major issues with speed and effectiveness. It is clear, however, that as presently constituted it is unable to resolve many of the major issues which face the profession. It has got involved with the political process and its final standards are no more than compromises between opposing views. The time taken to tackle important issues is unacceptable and in my view the ASC is incapable of responding efficiently to newly emerging issues. I believe that some of these problems are to do with the present structure and constitution of the ASC, but others need outside help.

I look forward to Sir Ronald Dearing's review of the present standard setting process and his subsequent recommendations. My own view is that we need a new body independent of the Consultative Committee of Accountancy Bodies. We need to include people of stature from both within and outside the profession. We need more energy and timeliness, more money and a stronger secretariat.

Above all, we need effective discipline and support from outside bodies who have the power. These include the profession, of course, but also the DTI, the Stock Exchange and the Inland Revenue.

Whatever the outcome, the time has come for the ASC to be given constitutional status separate from the accounting bodies. Such ties may have had their use in the past; today they can no longer be justified. They simply mean that the ASC continues to be embroiled in political and financial issues that are really the concern of the accounting bodies. As long as this is so, its full potential will not be achieved.

THE ROLE OF GOVERNMENT

A more direct and timely involvement by the government would be beneficial. The government should not, cannot and does not seek a direct role in setting accounting and professional standards. Its role is to ensure that the profession is responsive to change. Rather like the market which the Institute lacks it should be continually challenging, prodding, provoking and encouraging the profession to act. Above all, the government must monitor progress so that necessary changes do not become long overdue and it must stop the debates from going on for decades as they have with the small-business audit issue and the integration of the profession.

One always needs caution when dealing with the government. Governments have many objectives and are sometimes tempted to go for a political solution rather than take a balanced view on all the arguments. The present government has sought to strengthen the regulatory environment and we should support such initiatives as long as the benefits of supervision are clear and adequately compensate for the extra burden of costs on the profession and the community.

CONCLUSION

The changes I suggest are not esoteric notions about where the profession might move in the long term. I have dealt with real issues that need addressing as a matter of urgency. Strong leadership is needed if our professional body is not to become a trade association. Both government and the profession have roles to play in resolving these issues.

A complex, rapidly changing society needs a strong accounting profession. That profession must attract and retain the kind of people who are capable of responding to growing challenges and rigours. The changes I propose should lead to a more robust profession, able to serve the growing needs of society.

There are both strengths and weaknesses in the present system. My suggestions for improvement should not deny the strengths which exist. With leadership and imagination, we can make our system impregnable from interference by others and fulfil our role as a leading profession. It requires commitment from us all – the individual practitioners who together constitute the profession – our profession.

REFERENCES

Department of Trade and Industry (1987) *Letter to the accountancy bodies accompanying regulation of auditors*, Consultative Document, DTI, London.

Institute of Chartered Accountants in England and Wales (1985) *Governing the Institute*, Report of a Working Party under the Chairmanship of Mr F.E. Worsley, ICAEW, London.

Office of Fair Trading (1986) *Restrictions on the kind of Organisations through which Members of Professions may offer their Services: A Report by the Director General of Fair Trading*, OFT, London.

6

Accounting standards and special purpose transactions – some lessons from taxation

GRAEME MACDONALD

Peter Bird had been interested in accounting standards since Professor Edward Stamp's attack on the accountancy profession's lack of standard practice (Stamp, 1969). Nearly twenty years later he had become concerned with what he termed 'standards avoidance'. By this term he meant transactions undertaken in such a way as to circumvent the requirements of certain accounting standards, come within others or generally change the message given by accounting statements. The artificial structuring of a takeover so as to allow merger accounting rather than require compliance with acquisition accounting is an example. The approach originally advocated by the profession in response to such activity was to adopt as an accounting policy a requirement to account for economic substance (ICAEW, 1985). The question of substance or form is one familiar to students of tax law, particularly with regard to cases of tax avoidance. As one who had always retained an academic interest in taxation, and with whom I have spent many happy years teaching the subject, Peter's solution to 'standards avoidance' was to follow the approach adopted by the House of Lords in recent tax cases (see particularly *Ramsay (WT) Ltd* v. *IRC* [1981] STC 174, *Furniss* v. *Dawson* [1984] STC 153 and *Craven* v. *White* [1988] STC 476). This approach did not involve acceptance of substance over form as a general principle but, rather, recognized that in the limited case of 'a series of inter-dependent transactions designed to produce a given result, it is . . . perfectly legitimate to draw a distinction between the substance and form of the composite transaction' (*Furniss* v. *Dawson* [1984] STC 153, 158). In such a case the courts would ignore for fiscal purposes such preordained transactions as were undertaken only for the purpose of avoiding tax. The United States Federal Courts have characterized such transactions as having no 'business purpose', a test which appealed to Peter in seeking to determine which transactions should be the subject of some special accounting treatment.

In the event the Accounting Standards Committee has produced Exposure Draft No. 42, *Accounting for Special Purpose Transactions* (ASC, 1988). It makes no distinction between transactions which have and have not a 'business purpose', but it does in some respects closely resemble the judgments in recent tax cases. Special purpose transactions are defined as those for which the accounting treatment differs:

> Depending on whether the elements are taken step by step or whether the transaction is viewed as a whole; (para. 56)

and the statement proposes that:

> Where a transaction is only one in a connected series, the substance of the series of transactions should be viewed as a whole. (para. 57)

The purpose of this piece is to compare in a speculative manner accounting avoidance and tax avoidance and to see whether from an experience of tax legislation we can learn anything of general benefit to accounting standards. (For a brief review of the issues discussed here see ASC (1981).)

STANDARDS AS LAW?

We must first recognize that tax policy is manifest in and enforced through laws. In discussion of tax policy it is all too easy to forget that citizens do not willingly pay tax even when the rationale for the tax is to finance the provision of public goods. Ideas as to what constitutes an efficient or fair tax have to be translated into work-able laws. Similarly public discussion of proposed accounting standards makes it clear that preparers of accounts do not always have an altruistic interest in what represents 'best' accounting practice. Like many discussants of proposed tax reform their concern is for themselves, seeking to ensure that standards accom-modate their interests. The response of recalcitrant taxpayers to tax laws is either to evade (ignore the law) or avoid (arrange within the law) tax. The law contains sanctions to penalize, and so deter, evasion, and has developed further laws aimed at combating avoid-ance, although as the recent cases referred to above show there is a limit to what generalized rules can achieve in this respect.

Reasons for evading or avoiding standards may vary from consid-erations of cost of compliance, perceptions of usefulness or desire to improve the accounting picture that would otherwise be presented. Whatever the motive it is clear that standards are evaded – non-compliance with the Current Cost Standard (SSAP 16) is an example. In a tax system the result of widespread evasion is collapse of the system; in the case of SSAP 16 the result was the demise of the standard and, possibly, long-term damage to the credibility of the accounting standard setting process. The problem of evasion for tax systems generally arises where there are genuine problems of administrative control – cash transactions are notoriously prob-lematic both for income tax and value added tax. Evasion of accounting standards raises nothing like the same problems: the numbers potentially involved are of a different order, the accounts themselves are public documents and they are subject to audit. Clearly either the sanctions available to the authorities are inadequate, or the authorities are not inclined to enforce them, or the standards in general or in particular contain overgenerous let-out clauses which are too readily used and accepted by auditors (see the Explanatory Foreword to Statements of Standard Accounting Practice).

Whatever the reason for non-compliance it seems that standards require more positive and stronger backing as being 'a right thing'. This would come most readily from recognition in the Companies Act (although the moral force of law is lost if the specific content is generally regarded as unacceptable). This suggestion is not new and the objections to it are varied, but two in particular are relevant here. The first is that to enshrine standards in law can limit flexibility and change; standards might become ossified through time because parliamentary procedure restricts the capacity to make timely changes. There are various solutions to this: one is to give general acceptance to standards through a compliance requirement in the Companies Act and to adopt particular standards through the medium of statutory instruments (e.g. under s. 256 of the Companies Act 1985). VAT legislation is an example of how changes can be made easily and speedily using this method of legislating (and is a useful weapon in counteracting the latest avoidance techniques). An alternative is to require compliance in the Act and delegate the power to issue standards to some authority established for the purpose. This raises the second objection to legislative backing for accounting standards – the question of who determines their content. While standards are created and enforced by the accountancy profession, albeit with input from other interested parties, this remains a matter of local government or self-regulation. However, once standards come within the realms of statute they are in the public domain and subject to much closer scrutiny. The issue becomes one not of professional expertise but public interest. The profession is ambivalent: it would probably like the general backing of the law along the lines suggested above, but, as experts, does not wish to lose control of the content of accounting standards.

Accounting standards have probably come too far now to remain a matter for local professional expertise. In fact we may now have the worst of all possible worlds with no general statutory recognition of accounting standards but with the effective adoption within the Companies Act of the content or ideas of some particular standards (see, for example, Schedules 4 and 5, Companies Act 1985, as regards accounting principles and associated companies respectively). An authority with delegated powers would be composed of representatives from a range of interest groups. It would not be regarded as an arm of the profession but it is unthinkable that the profession would not have a considerable input both formally and informally. Such an authority would have powers to issue, review and change accounting standards and would be charged with the responsibility for enforcing compliance. Let us suppose that an Accounting Standards Board (ASB) is established under a Companies Act.

84

STANDARDS AND COMPLIANCE

How would the existence of the ASB help in the question of 'standards avoidance'? In one sense it might make avoidance more widespread in that non-compliance (evasion) would be less feasible in the face of legal sanctions and more effective policing. But this ignores a more basic question: why do preparers of accounts wish to evade or avoid compliance with standards? As noted above the costs of compliance might be regarded as outweighing the benefits, a common argument used in defence of not adopting current cost accounting in times of relatively low inflation. A response to this might be similar to that used in discussing the limited recognition of inflation in the tax system: that a present low rate of inflation does not obviate the need for a system which is capable of coping with high inflation (given that the need for adjustment is demonstrable), and that to recognize it for some purposes (capital gains tax) and not others (income tax) is inefficient and inequitable. In other words accounting for inflation (and/or price changes) is of such general importance over the long term that this should be complied with notwithstanding the short-term balance between costs and benefits. At the other extreme non-compliance might be attractive because preparers can represent a state of affairs (and themselves as directors) more advantageously by not complying. Whether such non-compliance would present a true and fair view is difficult to assess in general terms because of the lack of abstract definition available to that term. However, we could argue that non-compliance of this sort could be misleading, not because it does not represent a true state of affairs in a 'correct' sense or a state of affairs which could reasonably be viewed as true, but because in comparison with other economic entities who have complied the non-complying company appears better (whereas on a standard basis it would not). Non-compliance of this sort, however achieved, would probably be considered unacceptable in the way that tax evasion or artificial avoidance of the Ramsay type was unacceptable.

However, in other cases preparers might consider a standard as inappropriate to their peculiar circumstances even though they quite clearly came within the letter of the standard (as explicitly recognized in the Explanatory Foreword but rejected in ASC (1981)).

There have been similar cases in the past involving tax avoidance legislation; innocent taxpayers, recognized by the courts as not within the mischief at which the section was aimed, have nevertheless found themselves unambiguously within its letter and thus taxed under the full rigours of the section (e.g. *IRC* v. *De Vigier* [1964] 42 TC 24). No help is available to the unwary unless the purpose is made explicit in the section (e.g. as in s. 739 (1), Taxes Act 1988). That statements of purpose should be used in legislation to delimit or clarify its scope and effect was recommended by the Renton Committee (Renton, 1975, para. 11.8), particularly with regard to fiscal legislation (para. 17.11), but this recommendation does not seem to have been heeded. Instead more recent anti-avoidance sections have protected the innocent non-avoider by including a clearance provision whereby the potential taxpayer may formally seek clearance so that disclosed transactions would not be taxed under the relevant section.

Such a procedure could apply to accounting standards. Preparers who on the basis of some criterion felt that a standard should not apply to their situation could apply to the ASB for clearance from compliance. The merit in this procedure is that it recognizes that standards, being rules, have to be generalizations, but that there will inevitably be situations to which the generalization is not, under agreed criteria, appropriate. The alternative approach of attempting to cover every foreseeable circumstance 'can result in very complex provisions that are not easy for even an expert legislative audience to comprehend' (Renton, 1975, para. 17.11). ED 42 has taken the general rather than the specific approach. As such, like widely drawn anti-avoidance legislation, it may not always be appropriate, but this is an argument available to the innocent and the avoider alike. Only a clearance procedure, operated at arm's length and not through the special relationship with the auditor, can properly distinguish between the two.

Furthermore a clearance procedure could improve the compliance climate: uncleared non-compliance would be seen to be without merit and heavily penalized, whereas general application of standards to inappropriate cases without the clearance option serves only to bring the standard into disrepute. Let us suppose then that preparers of accounting statements can apply to the ASB for clearance from the requirement to comply with a standard in stated circumstances.

A CONCEPTUAL FRAMEWORK

How would the ASB decide whether or not to give clearance? Clearly its deliberations would require some criteria, a reference point, even a conceptual framework – 'a structure for thinking about what is "better" accounting and financial reporting' (Macve, 1981, p. 9). The qualitative characteristics of accounting information as developed by FASB (1980) would seem to provide an appropriate model giving 'a number of generalizations or guidelines for making accounting choices' (para. 11). The hierarchy of accounting qualities outlined in the FASB statement recognizes that 'the relative weight to be given to different qualities must vary according to circumstances' (para. 34). Ideally an accounting standard would start with a statement of purpose and scope (following Renton) clarifying which qualities in particular the standard seeks to elaborate. For example, a standard on extraordinary and exceptional items might state that whilst meeting other qualities its primary aim is to increase predictive value by disaggregating recurrent items from non-recurrent items.

In considering an application for clearance the ASB would consider whether in all the circumstances the proposed departure would either better meet the objective of the standard, or would provide significantly better information overall (taking into account other information qualities) even though perhaps providing 'worse' information in respect of the particular standard from which clearance is sought. In other words the ASB would have to weigh the qualities, which might well conflict, in the context of the particular circumstances, circumstances possibly not considered by the draftsman. Clearance would be the exception rather than the rule, and would apply predominantly where compliance in peculiar circumstances would result in 'worse' information. By providing for clearance the standard setter can be bolder, particularly in respect of standards aimed at 'narrowing the areas of difference and variety in accounting practice' (ICAEW, 1969). By operating a clearance procedure the standard setting process could become more dynamic

– a common set of circumstances not envisaged by the standard setter would quickly become evident and could lead to an amended or additional standard. Such changes would represent a considered response to changed or unforeseen circumstances on the basis of well-recognized criteria rather than an unprincipled surrender to the pressures of a particular interest group.

Finally the adoption of a conceptual framework might give some substance to the notion of a true and fair view. Hitherto clearance from complying with accounting standards has effectively depended on being able to do so in the interests of presenting a true and fair view. Yet there has been no definitive statement of what we might understand by that term even though it has been enshrined in company law for forty years and has now passed into the vocabulary of European Community Directives. Whilst we should not expect 'true and fair view' to be replaced by a hierarchy of accounting qualities, it does not seem unreasonable that an audit report, in averring to a true and fair view, should be understood to be using a summary term which indicates that accounts have been prepared and reviewed in the light of generally recognized accounting qualities. The audit report, however, should be where 'true and fair' stays; with clearance and with a conceptual framework there would seem no place for it in standards.

AVOIDANCE – SUBSTANCE OR FORM?

How far does any of this help us with the 'standards avoidance' that concerned Peter Bird? In part clearance will obviate the need for avoidance – but only if the application is expected to be successful. Otherwise, given more effective enforcement measures, the pull of avoidance as opposed to evasion might be stronger. Consider again the group wishing to take advantage of merger accounting. This is tantamount to the taxpayer seeking to take advantage of a tax exemption for which he initially does not qualify. In terms of tax policy one answer to this type of problem is to have a clean tax base free of exemption and reliefs. In the accounting example the easy solution would be either to outlaw merger accounting completely or allow its wholesale adoption. There may be valid objections to either solution but in any event the easy solution does not resolve the general issue:

how do we account for transactions which have only been undertaken, or been undertaken in a particular form, so as to result in an accounting statement which is materially different from that which would obtain had the transaction not been undertaken, or undertaken differently – transactions the purpose of which is to change the accounting message?

As noted above the accountancy profession's initial response of adopting a general policy of preferring substance over form has been modified. The issue of substance or form is also one which has arisen in tax cases over the years, with form holding sway until recent House of Lords decisions. However, even now any preference for substance is not a general canon of construction but is confined to avoidance cases, and then only in limited situations (see *Craven* v. *White* [1988] STC 476 for the limits). In general the position remains that enunciated in *Duke of Westminster* v. *IRC* (19 TC, 490):

> In order to ascertain the substance, I must look at the legal effect of the bargain which the parties have entered into . . .
> (At 521)

and:

> The substance of the transaction . . . is . . . to be found and to be found only by ascertaining their respective rights and liabilities under the deed.   (At 524)

The approach of ED 42 to substance seems to reflect this position:

> Accounting for substance is explained in the statement as meaning that a transaction's accounting treatment should fairly reflect its commercial effect.   (1.15)

and:

> It is analysis of the commercial effects flowing from the form of special purpose transactions that will lead to an understanding of their substance.   (1.16)

As with the tax avoidance decisions it is the circumstances of special purpose transactions being part of a composite whole that leads to an overall view, as opposed to a step-by-step view, being taken of the substance.

For accounting purposes it seems difficult to sustain a general preference for substance because it is not clear that in any situation there would be agreement as to what constituted economic substance. A capitalist economy depends on there being clearly defined exclusive legal rights. To be able to ignore these in some undefined circumstances in the interest of reflecting true economic substance solves no problems; at best it presents the problem in another guise – what is the economic substance: at worst it opens up a host of possible inconsistencies which accounting standards are designed to avoid.

In fact the solution to some accounting problems does not require the panacea of substance; all that may be required is a change in the way accounting rules deal with legal form. For example, the treatment of finance leases whereby assets leased but not owned are shown as assets and the rental obligations under the lease as a corresponding liability arguably involves an adjustment to accounting conventions more than a flouting of legal form. The legal rights and obligations under a lease are respectively legal assets and liabilities. It is accounting conventions which lead to a balance sheet which excludes some assets merely because there is no unexpired cost attributable to them. To include such assets in the balance sheet is to recognize their legal existence, and to value them at the cost of the underlying asset as being a conservative estimate of economic present value seems unexceptionable; to exclude them has been found to be undesirable in terms of quality of information. ED 42 effectively recognizes that the weakness is in the accounting rules in that it has to face up to the conceptual question of what constitutes an asset for accounting purposes.

However, there is an instance, generally well defined, where substance does rule (or at least legal form does not) without comment – consolidated accounts. The accounting solution (which pre-dated legal requirements) is to ignore legal form, under which shares are only legal interests in a company and *not* legal interests in the assets of the company, and account as if the assets of the subsidiary were those of the parent. This represents a pragmatic solution to a well-defined problem which became best practice and acquired the backing of law. It did not involve the wholesale adoption of a general preference for substance over form.

However, having denied the need for general recourse to a doctrine of substance over form it has to be recognized that this will be the implicit solution to certain strictly defined problems. As noted above it is implicit in consolidated accounts. It is also implicit in much tax avoidance legislation which uses the technique of 'deeming' something which is not the case to be the case; or, to use the language of the Law Society (1986), it 'recharacterizes' certain transactions. This seems a wholly appropriate reaction to certain tax avoidance schemes and seems equally acceptable in cases of accounting 'window-dressing' which equate with artificial avoidance schemes. However, while it might be acceptable within a recognized legislative framework one can understand the objections to one profession with no legal authority taking it upon itself to deem what shall be what. We are driven back to the conclusion that there needs to be a legally backed authority to whom the powers of standard setting are delegated. We could then expect not only specific standards dealing with accounting abuses but also, another technique from tax legislation, extended definitions of such terms as subsidiary, control and associate for accounting purposes, and the use of notions of connected persons and associated operations.

CONCLUSION

There is, perhaps, something to be learned from a broad comparison of tax legislation and accounting standards. To be maintained a tax system requires legal enforcement; it cannot rely on willing co-operation. Tax evasion and avoidance are a testament to this. If accounting standards are to be taken seriously and enforced then non-compliance cannot be tolerated on any significant scale. The advent of 'standards avoidance' and the increasing use of sophisticated devices to distort accounting messages, together with the measures necessary to counteract these practices, suggests that if accounting standards are to be maintained in the long term then they will need to be backed by the force of law. Further, if standards are to be applied, interpreted and developed as law then there is a case for developing a set of criteria or a conceptual framework by reference to which they can be seen to operate. Exposure Draft 42 explicitly recognizes for the first time the need to appeal to accounting concepts (ASC, 1988, preface 1.12). In developing this exposure draft the ASC has taken a quasi-judicial role and issued a pronouncement strikingly similar to those of the House of Lords in recent tax avoidance cases. Their Lordships argued that their approach to closely integrated situations was an affirmation of the true judicial process, and that determining the acceptable limits to tax avoidance is beyond the power of the blunt instrument of legislation and remains to be probed and determined judicially. In ED 42 the Accounting Standards Committee is exercising a similar function but without the authority vested in the Law Lords (who, some would argue, have exceeded their authority as regards tax law). The accounting problems faced are real enough and require answering, but they may only be the tip of the iceberg. It is time we recognized that standards are intended to be laws and provided the legal machinery to enforce those laws and resolve difficult cases.

REFERENCES

ASC (1981) *Setting Accounting Standards,* Report and Recommendations by the Accounting Standards Committee, ASC, London.

ASC (1988) *Accounting for Special Purpose Transactions,* Exposure Draft No. 42 of the Accounting Standards Committee, ASC, London.

FASB (1980) *Qualitative Characteristics of Accounting Information,* Statement of Financial Accounting Concepts No. 2, Financial Accounting Standards Board, Stamford, Connecticut.

ICAEW (1969) *Statement of Intent on Accounting Standards in the 1970s,* Institute of Chartered Accountants in England and Wales, London.

ICAEW (1985) *Off Balance Sheet Finance and Window Dressing,* Technical Release 603, Institute of Chartered Accountants in England and Wales, London.

The Law Society (1986) *Off Balance Sheet Finance and Window Dressing,* Memorandum by the Society's Standing Committee on Company Law, The Law Society, London.

Macve, R. (1981) *A Conceptual Framework for Financial Accounting and Reporting,* Institute of Chartered Accountants in England and Wales, London.

Renton (1975) *The Preparation of Legislation,* Cmnd 6053, HMSO, London.

Stamp, E. (1969) Auditing the auditors, *The Times,* 11 September.

7

Accounting basics: language, writing materials, numerals and calculation

R.H. PARKER

Accounting is the recording of economic events (Sorter, 1969). Which events to record and what monetary amounts (if any) to assign to them are conceptual matters of great importance about which there is no consensus, but the existence of accounting is fortunately not dependent upon such consensus. Once it has been decided what events to record it is necessary to decide how to record them. Accountants can, for example, provide:

1. A chronological listing of events (a 'journal') to which may be added;
2. A further classification of events into categories (a 'ledger');
3. On the other hand they may, making no assumptions about users' needs, store data about events without any attempt to order or classify them routinely (a 'database approach').

Whichever is chosen there are further decisions to make. These concern the language in which the accounts are written, writing materials and implements, the numerals used and aids to calculation. It is the last set of questions that are discussed, in a historical context, in the present paper. These decisions are not trivial but are basic to all accounting. Without language, writing materials, numerals and calculating aids accounting could exist only in the most primitive form.

When the first institutes of professional accountants were established in the nineteenth century, book-keepers in Britain typically maintained accounts on paper in bound books, written in English with a steel-nibbed pen, using Arabic numerals which they added up without any mechanical calculating aid. Five hundred years earlier, in the fourteenth century, manorial accountants typically kept their records on parchment rolls, written in Latin with a quill pen, and using Roman numerals which they added up on a line abacus or counting board. Late-twentieth-century accountants in Britain have completely abandoned parchment, Latin and the abacus but still, on occasion, keep their accounts on paper in bound books, albeit using a biro or a fountain pen. But twentieth-century book-keeping machines, punched card installations and electromechanical calculating machines are already museum pieces. The computers that British accountants increasingly use produce an output which is in English, uses Arabic numerals and is usually on paper but these are purely for convenience. Computers could, if accountants so wished, produce accounts in Latin, printed on parchment and employing Roman numerals.

The purpose of this paper is to trace the languages, writing materials, numerals and calculating aids used in British accounting and how and why these have changed over time. The hypothesis of the paper is that the changes have arisen from assessments of costs v. benefits which have depended on (1) who kept the accounts, (2) for whom, and (3) for what purpose. Consider, at one extreme, a merchant (assumed to be male) who keeps his own accounts and keeps them solely for his own use. Such a merchant is likely to keep accounts in the language he understands and writes best (in the simplest case he may be proficient in only one language), in the most convenient material that comes to hand, using the numeral system that he finds easiest, and employing such calculating aids as are readily available and within his competence.

At the other extreme the accounts may be kept by a trained clerk working for the manager of a business whose accounts must be submitted to (and perhaps audited by) an outside owner or tax collector or both. In this case it is less easy to predict what language, writing material, numerals and calculating aids will be used. This will depend on the relative power of the parties concerned (who can, of course, be regarded as in agency relationships with each other). The clerk, for example, will have little incentive to change a familiar language of account (say Latin) to that of the manager or outside user, since he (the clerk) will incur costs but may not reap any benefits. It will be necessary for the manager or outsider to provide such benefits (e.g. continued employment instead of loss of job) to persuade the clerk to make the change. Conflict is not inevitable. In many cases it may be in the interest of all three parties to make a change (or at least not to oppose it).

Language, writing materials, numerals and aids to calculation are all interrelated but for purposes of exposition are discussed here in sequence.

LANGUAGES OF ACCOUNT

Britain has never been a wholly monolingual country. As well as English in its various forms numerous Celtic languages have been spoken and Latin and French have also played crucial roles (Price, 1984). The dominance of English is a relatively recent development (Baugh, 1957; Barber, 1976, Chapter 2). During the Romano-British period the official language south of the imperial frontier was Latin. Celtic languages were also in use but it is not known for certain which language most people spoke most of the time (Price, 1984, Chapter 12). From the fifth century AD Britain was settled by Angles, Saxons, Jutes and Danes and until the Norman Conquest of 1066 the most widespread language was Anglo-Saxon or Old English. After the Conquest English remained the most widely spoken language but until the fourteenth century the language of the ruling class was Norman French. By the fourteenth century English had won its way back into universal use as the spoken language; those who could speak French were bilingual. Changes in the relative importance of the written languages took longer. Chaucer's *Canterbury Tales*, the major literary work of Middle English, dates from the 1380s. The earliest private letters extant in English were written in the 1390s. The *Paston Letters* (1422–1509) were written in French before the mid 1420s but thereafter almost entirely in English (Kingsford, 1925, pp. 22–4).

For non-literary and most public purposes English, as a written language, had to compete with Latin, the language of the Church and hence also of administration and scholarship, as well as French. In the early Middle Ages, to be literate was to be able to read and write Latin, which remained the language of European scholarship until well into the seventeenth century. It is the language, for example, of Newton's *Principia Mathematica* (1686–87).

The language of the law was also slow to change (Baker, 1979). Most of the literature of English law before the seventeenth century was written either in French or in Latin. A statute (in French) of 1362, enjoining the use of English in lawsuits, marked an official recognition of English, although it may have had little effect in practice. The decisions of the courts were recorded in Latin. Law French was abolished during the Commonwealth (1650–60) but revived at the Restoration. Parliament finally ended the use of Latin and French in legal proceedings in 1731. In Scotland (which was subject to Norman influence but not a Conquest) Latin was used for charters, but otherwise from the earliest times Scots (which gradually became closer to standard English) was used (Walker, 1980).

This is the background against which to consider the surviving British accounting records. The earliest evidence we have of writing in Britain are the writing tablets uncovered at the Roman fort of Vindolanda, which date from around AD 100, a decade or two before the fort became part of Hadrian's Wall. The tablets, which are, of course, in Latin, include a number of documents recording the receipt of food and drink (including substantial quantities of beer for the soldiers on the frontier) (Bowman and Thomas, 1983; Bowman, 1983).

No further accounting records are known in Britain until the twelfth and thirteenth centuries. The central government's pipe rolls (Johnson, 1925) begin in 1130–31; the first written accounts of the large ecclesiastical institutions such as Canterbury Cathedral Priory and the bishopric of Winchester date from the first decade of the thirteenth century; manorial accounts start to become common in the 1270s and 1280s (Harvey, 1984, p. 25).

All these accounts were written up in Latin as was also the first (*c.* 1179) treatise on government accounting: the *Dialogus de Scaccario* (Dialogue of the Exchequer) by Richard, son of Nigel, Treasurer of England (Johnson, 1983). The thirteenth- and fourteenth-century didactic treatises on estate management, however, of which the most notable was Walter of Henley's *Husbandry*, were written in French, the language of the stewards and bailiffs responsible for the management of manorial estates. Double-entry book keeping arrived too late in Britain for works on the subject to be written in Latin or French but a number of them (notably Liset's *Amphitalami*, 1660; Every's *Speculum mercativum*, 1673; Colinson's *Idea rationaria*, 1683; Jones's *Diarium mercatoris, c.* 1770; and Hawkins's *Clavis comercii*, 1718) have Latin short titles (Parker, 1984a, p. 111).

Until the sixteenth century Latin was also the usual language of the accounts kept by households and estates with occasional lapses into English or French where, presumably, the writer did not know or could not recall the appropriate Latin word (Myatt-Price, 1956, p. 100; Wood-Legh, 1956, xiii–xiv). An interesting fifteenth-century example which has been printed (Myers, 1985, Chapter 5) is the household accounts of Queen Joan of Navarre (wife of Henry IV and stepmother of Henry V) during her imprisonment by her step-son for alleged treason by means of witchcraft, 1419–21. The accounts are in Latin but in inventory of Queen Joan's valuables in the custody of Friar John Randolf, August 1419, is extant in English, French and Latin, although the three versions are not entirely in agreement with each other. The account rolls of a fifteenth-century iron master working iron on the estates of the Bishop of Durham are also in Latin, although extremely faulty (Lapsley, 1899).

The late-sixteenth-century and early-seventeenth-century estate and household accounts of the Earls of Northumberland reprinted by James (1955) and Batho (1962) are mainly in English but some estate accounts for 1581 are in Latin. The accounts of the Roberts family of Boarzell, Sussex, *c.* 1568–82, are in English (Tittler, 1977), as are those of the Sidney ironworks (also in Sussex) for the years 1541–73 (Crossley, 1975), although the latter contain a few Latin phrases such as *ut supra* (as above) and *hoc anno* (this year).

The accounts of English boroughs, Scots burghs and the London guilds and livery companies are in Latin until the fifteenth century when French and English start to take over. In Hull, for example, the rental of the town's land was kept in Latin until 1465 and in English thereafter (Horrox, 1983, p. 111).

The accounts of private merchants are less likely to survive than those of the great institutions of the State and the Church. The earliest extant are those of the wool merchant William de la Pole from the 1330s (Fryde, 1964), of the London merchant Gilbert Maghfeld from the 1390s (Rickert, 1926–27), and of the Cely family of merchants from the fifteenth century (Hanham, 1985). The earliest sixteenth-century mercantile ledgers which have survived are those of Andrew Halyburton (1492–1503) (see Innes, 1867; Ritson, 1966) and Thomas Howell (1522–27) (see Connell-Smith, 1950). The de la Pole accounts are in Latin, the Maghfeld accounts in French and the Cely accounts are mainly in English. Halyburton's ledger is in Scots English. Howell's and all other surviving ledgers from Tudor England are in English.

Not all merchants resident in England had English or French as their native language. Italian merchants such as the London branches of the Gallerani Company of Siena (1305–08) and the Borromeo Company of Milan (1436–39) kept their accounts in Italian (Nobes, 1982; K[ats], 1926).

English is not quite, even in the twentieth century, the universal language of accounting in Britain. Company law makes provision for 'Welsh companies' some of which no doubt keep their accounting records in Welsh. The Companies Act 1985 does not prescribe the language in which accounting records must be kept. Nor does it proscribe the filing with the Registrar of Companies of financial statements in Welsh or any other language. Such statements must, however, be accompanied by a certified translation into English.

Multinational companies reporting to an international audience need to choose the language or languages in which to report. With English established as the international language of business few British multinationals feel a need to translate their annual reports into other languages. The exceptions include the two Anglo-Dutch multinationals Shell and Unilever.

To what extent do the choices actually made of languages of account support the explanatory hypothesis put forward in the previous section? The clerks who were trained in medieval England to keep accounts for Church, State, household and manor were taught to do so in Latin (Richardson, 1941) and there would have been no benefit to them to do so in French or English. Those who have learned a complicated task and a set of technical terms in one language are unlikely voluntarily to choose to change to another. Custom and the self-interest of the clerks made change very slow. As Jenkinson (1926) points out:

> . . . The principal varieties of [accounts] which have survived, the public ones . . . and the private ones dealing with the administration of land or . . . with that of great households, attained fixed forms at a very early date in the medieval period; and, convention acting as strongly here as elsewhere, these forms lingered on outwardly unchanged for many centuries.
> (pp. 264–5)

The most extreme example of unwillingness to change comes from the English exchequer. The wording on exchequer tallies (discussed below) and in the Receipt Books (into which the tally inscriptions were copied) remained in Latin right up to the end: tally-making ceased in 1826; the Receipt Books lasted until 1834 (Jenkinson, 1911, p. 377–8; Jenkinson, 1925, p. 309).

Whilst the language of the manorial account remained Latin the language of treatises on estate management depended on the preferred language of the managers. In the words of Oschinsky (1971), who distinguishes in effect between principals and agents:

> The use of French and Latin shows a distinct pattern. The account, an administrative record written by clerks since its first appearance, was always in Latin, and the treatises on the form of the account, compiled for the use of clerks, were likewise in Latin. The language spoken by seignorial lords, or their stewards, was French and so was the language of the earliest treatise on estate management compiled for the lord of a lay estate, the *Rules*. The language of the Church was Latin and therefore even rules on estate management and ordinances concerning monastic households or estates were written in Latin.
> (p. 9)

The language of mercantile accounts was more varied. Custom had not laid down which language to use nor was there a profession of trained clerks writing only in Latin. The accounts of de la Pole are presumably in Latin because they record information supplied for the use of the Court of Exchequer (Fryde, 1964, p. IX : 7). Those of Maghfeld are in French perhaps because that language (even if Maghfeld, who may have been a model for Chaucer's merchant, spoke it, like Chaucer's prioress, 'after the scole of Stratford atte Bowe') was the one that the merchant, whose accounts were solely for his own use, wrote best. The Celys were wool merchants trading extensively with France but during a period when French was becoming a foreign language in England. Again, they presumably chose English as the language that they wrote best. So far as later merchants were concerned, English had become the common language of communication. By the sixteenth century there was no reason for an English merchant to keep his accounts in any other language. By the same token, there was no reason, until the corporate disclosure laws of the twentieth century, for foreign merchants operating in Britain not to keep their accounts in their own vernacular.

WRITING MATERIALS AND IMPLEMENTS

Written accounting, as distinct from oral accounting, comes into being when accounts are recorded with a writing implement on some form of writing material. All imaginable types of material have at various times and places been used for writing on (Gaur, 1987, p. 35). In Britain the most important have been wood, parchment and paper (the last for many centuries imported rather than manufactured locally). Both parchment and paper can be made up into either 'rolls' or 'codices', i.e. books not in roll form, or, to the modern user, simply 'books'.

For the Roman soldiers at Vindolanda the traditional materials were papyrus and wood, the latter in the form of tablets either whitened to receive ink from a reed pen or, more usually, covered with wax in which writing could be scratched with a stylus. This could then be obliterated if necessary and the tablet used again. A set of tablets, pierced at the edges and held together by thongs was termed, amongst other things, a codex (Croix, 1956, Appendix B). There is no evidence that papyrus was used at Vindolanda (although it was common throughout the Roman Empire). Some wooden tablets have been found but much more common, and perhaps used as a substitute for papyrus in an area where that material was difficult and expensive to obtain, were thin slices or leaves of wood (birch or alder) made to take writing in ink. An account of food supplies, for example, consists of a series of wooden leaves folded across the middle and tied to one another, forming a concertina type of wooden notebook and providing a convenient way of presenting accounts consisting of long narrow columns.

The obvious writing materials and implements for accountants in the predominantly rural environment of medieval Britain were wood, parchment and feathers (the English word 'pen' is derived from the Latin *penna,* feather). Wood was readily available in what was then a heavily forested country. Parchment is made from the skin of an animal (sheep, goat, cow or calf) and:

> Although never very plentiful it was always made available by the autumn slaughter of animals, which was necessitated by the lack of winter feeding stuff.
>
> (Whalley, 1980, p. viii.)

The quill pen superseded the Roman reed pen because it was more easily obtainable in Western Europe. Goose feathers (those most preferred) were not difficult to find when every village had its own pond (Whalley, 1975, pp. 29–30; 1980, p. viii).

Waxed wooden tablets continued to be used for calculations not intended to be kept permanently. The major use of wood, however, was for tallies. A tally was a notched stick used as a record of a receipt or a payment. Notches of various sizes were cut to represent various amounts. The amount of money received or paid was written on the tally in Roman numerals and Latin words. The tally was then split lengthwise into two segments of unequal size: the 'stock' and the 'foil'. Tallies were extensively used in government, manorial and mercantile accounting and probably predate the Norman Conquest (Johnson, 1983). The author of the *Dialogus de Scaccario* describes as follows the method of cutting them:

> A thousand pounds are shown by a cut at the top of the tally wide enough to hold the thickness of the palm of the hand, a hundred that of the thumb, twenty pounds that of the little finger, a pound that of a swelling barley-corn, a shilling smaller,

but enough for the two cuts to make a small notch. A penny is indicated by a single cut without removing any of the wood.

(Johnson, 1983, p. 23.)

Private tallies probably reached their greatest popularity in the late thirteenth and early fourteenth centuries. Jenkinson (1925) conjectures that:

About the year 1350 old-fashioned officials would be grumbling that in their day the scratch of a knife on a slip of hazel was good enough for any man, but every knave who sold a few oats for the king's service must have parchment and ink and wax to content him. (p. 314)

Tallies undoubtedly had great virtues: they were durable, cheap, easy to understand and not only provided 'a sophisticated and practical record of numbers' but 'were more convenient to keep and store than parchments, less complex to make, and no easier to forge' (Clanchy, 1979, p. 96). To most persons in medieval England tallies were no doubt preferable to words they could not read, written on more expensive parchment. They continued to be used by the Exchequer, however, well after the conditions appropriate to their use had passed away. Roger North (1714) describes them as being 'of ordinary Use in Keeping Accounts with illiterate people', points out that 'the Pen, and the Dr and Cr. Method have the Possession of all the Accounting Trade elsewhere' and denounces the Officers of the Exchequer who 'for their own Ends use it' and continue 'obsolete Ways and Forms . . . to the vast Oppression of the People, that have to do amongst them'.

The use of Exchequer tallies continued, amazingly, until 1826. In 1834 their end came at last. Used as fuel to heat the Houses of Parliament they started a fire that almost completely destroyed the Parliament buildings (Parker, 1984b).

To nineteenth-century observers tallies were a primitive survival from a preliterate past and there was no protest at their destruction. To Charles Dickens in 1855 speaking to the Administrative Reform Association the unwillingness of the Court of Exchequer to update its writing materials to 'pens, ink and paper, slates and pencils' had been a supreme example of an 'obstinate adherence to rubbish which time has long outlived' (Fielding, 1960, pp. 205–6).

The attitude to parchment was different. As Clanchy (1979, p. 96) points out, tallies were in a writing medium, wood, 'which was too uncouth for scholars to appreciate'. The same scholars were simultaneously taking pains to preserve medieval records kept on parchment.

Parchment as a writing material has never lacked admirers. It has been described as 'the most beautiful and suitable material for writing or printing that has ever been used' (Diringer, 1953, p. 170), and:

> The finest writing material ever devised by man. It is immensely strong, remains flexible indefinitely under normal conditions, does not deteriorate with age, and possesses a smooth, even surface which is both pleasant to the eye and provides unlimited scope for the finest writing and illumination. Above all, it . . . could be produced wherever the skins of suitable animals were available in sufficient quantity.
>
> (Roberts and Skeat, 1983, p. 8.)

Other advantages are easy stitching and high tearing strength. On the other hand parchment is relatively expensive and difficult to produce. It differs from leather in that it is prepared from wet, unhaired and limed animal skin by drying at ordinary temperatures whilst being stretched at the same time. Originally the best type of parchment, known as vellum, was made from calfskin, but the term is now applied to any type of parchment that is both thin and strong (Reed, 1972, pp. 5–6, Chapter 5).

By the sixteenth century paper had replaced parchment as the most common writing material used in Britain. The essential quality of paper (distinguishing it from papyrus) is that it is fabricated from macerated vegetable fibres (Hunter, 1957, p. 6). It was first made in China in c AD 105, but there were no paper mills anywhere in Europe until the twelfth century or in England before 1495. By 1720 England was producing about two-thirds of its total paper consumption but from the thirteenth century onwards it had been an imported manufacture – at first mainly from Italy and later from France and the Netherlands (Coleman, 1958, Chapter 1).

From the late fifteenth century the demand for paper was stimulated by the growth of printing. Parchment proved to be too limited in supply and too expensive for the growing number of printed books. For example, 180 copies of Gutenberg's 42-line Bible (1452–56) were printed on paper, and 30 on parchment. For *each* parchment copy, consisting of 641 leaves, the skins of more than 300 sheep were required (Plant, 1974, p. 190). Moreover, paper could be made more quickly, was lighter in weight, and, in its better qualities, almost as tough (Harrison, 1943, p. 79). During the fifteenth and sixteenth centuries the price of paper fell and that of parchment rose (Coleman, 1958, p. 7; Hills, 1988, p. 38).

Paper began to be used for accounting purposes from the fourteenth century, when it was used for the accounts of Bridport, Southampton, Hythe and other boroughs (Jenkins, 1900). The mid fifteenth-century household accounts of the Munden's Chantry, Bridport, were also kept on imported paper, although bound in vellum (Wood-Legh, 1956, p. xxxiv). The Cromwell household accounts (1417–76) were similarly kept in paper books (Myatt-Price, 1956). Paper did not oust parchment in the sixteenth and seventeenth centuries. The engrossed (i.e. the fair copy) accounts of the chamberlains (chief executives) of the City of London were written on parchment but the drafts were on paper (Masters, 1984, pp. ix, xxxix).

The decision whether to use paper rather than parchment appears to have been reached mainly on the grounds of availability and relative costs. The use of parchment was firmly established in the twelfth and thirteenth centuries and it was long regarded as the appropriate material for formal records (Clanchy, 1979). The intended user also appears to have been important. Putting it another way, the choice of writing material was apparently sometimes dependent upon 'the relative solemnity of the account' (Glénisson, in Dhondt, 1964, p. 179). Accounts intended only for internal use were more likely to be kept on paper. Those intended for submission externally were often kept on parchment.

Apart from deciding whether or not to write on parchment or paper, accountants had to decide whether to adopt the roll form or the codex form. This did not depend on the use of writing material: both parchment and paper can be made up without difficulty into either rolls or codices.

The possible relative advantages of the codex over the roll include economy, compactness, convenience of use, and ease of reference; those of the rolls over the codex, flexibility, no need for binding, and less need to plan ahead (cf. Roberts and Skeat, 1983, Chapter 9). Each advantage is discussed briefly below.

The codex can be regarded as more economic in that both sides of the material are used. Both sides of a roll can be used (and some-times were: the *dorse* of a manorial account roll was used to record movements of commodities) but there is a danger of effacement since the roll is unbound. The codex is more compact than the roll and easier to stack and shelve. This, however, may not have been seen as a great advantage when neither rolls nor codices existed in great quantities. The codex is more convenient to use since two hands are needed to hold a roll, one to unwind a convenient length, the other to roll up the portion already used. Equally, however, a codex also requires two hands, unless the book is rested on a desk or table. It is easier to locate a particular passage in a codex than in a roll.

The roll is more flexible, since extra membranes can readily be sewn on if desired to extend a roll. Rolls need no binding and have survived for many centuries without them. Binding, as a skilled operation, involves expense and delay whilst the binding is being executed. Compared with a roll, a codex involves a number of planning problems, such as calculating space ahead and laying out sheets and keeping them in the right order.

Of the accounts discussed so far in this paper, pipe rolls were, as their name suggests, kept in roll form, as also, typically, were the accounts of ecclesiastical institutions and manors. Household accounts were often kept in codex form. The Cromwell household accounts consist both of books (codices) and rolls, with the latter used only for the annual accounts (Myatt-Price, 1956).

The choice between rolls and codices was not clear-cut. Medieval England was, in fact, alone in Europe in its general preference for rolls. The reasons remain a mystery, but once rolls had been adopted bureaucracy ensured that they remained unchanged for centuries (Clanchy, 1979, p. 111).

The choice between rolls and codices has arisen in a new form in the computer age. It is the choice between serial access and random access.

Until the twentieth century most merchants' ledgers were in the form of bound books. Indeed in languages other than English the ledger is usually referred to as the great book. Yamey (1961) quotes Weddington (1567) as writing of the 'great boke or lidger', Peele (1569) of the 'leager or greate booke' and Malynes (1622) as contrasting the journal with a 'bigger book, called a Leiger, because the same remaineth (as lying) accordingly in a place for that purpose'.

It was within these bound ledgers that double-entry *book*-keeping took place. At first each account was ruled by hand but about 1770, according to Hunter (1957, p. 502), the first machine came into use in the UK for the ruling of paper for account-books. Ledgers remained bound books until the invention of the loose-leaf ledger in the United States in the 1880s and 1890s (Stoeckel, 1946). This provided not only an alternative to the bound ledger but was essential to the later introduction of accounting machinery. At the other extreme, the private ledger equipped with lock and key has also been claimed as an American invention of the 1880s (Littleton, 1946, pp. 459–60).

Loose-leaf ledgers reached the UK by the turn of the century. The great advantage of loose-leaf, or more generally, 'bookkeeping without books' or the 'slip system', as Dicksee (1911, Chapter XVIII) called it, was that it allowed entries of, for example, sales, to be made in invoices, sales day books and sales ledgers without 'continual recopying'. The system was dependent upon the use of carbon paper which was also a nineteenth-century invention (Delgado, 1979, Chapter 5). By the fourth edition (1911) of his standard text on *Advanced Accounting*, Dicksee felt bold enough to assert that the slip system was:

> now well past the experimental stage; that it has been used, with very excellent results, by a large number of well-known business houses for several years past; and that its use has given every satisfaction. (p. 220)

The dominance of *books* of account was for long reflected in the wording of British company legislation. Section 436 of the Companies Act 1948, however, provided that the law could be satisfied 'either by making entries in bound books or by recording the matters in question in any other manner'. The Companies Act 1976, s. 12

106

(now Companies Act 1985, s. 722) substituted the phrase 'account-ing records' for bound books. The Auditing Practices Committee of the Consultative Committee of Accountancy Bodies sought in 1977 counsel's opinion on the meaning of the new term. Their opinion was that:

> Accounting records comprise the orderly collection and identi-fication of the information in question, rather than a mere accumulation of documents. The accounting records need not be in book form, they may take the form of, for example, a loose-leaf binder or computer tape. It will even be sufficient if the books of prime entry are in the form of a secure clip of invoices with an add-list attached. The essence of the matter is that the information recorded is organized and labelled so as to be capable of retrieval. A carrier-bag full of invoices will not suffice.
>
> *(True and Fair* (Winter 1977/78), 6.)

As discussed below, as computer systems have developed, paper has ceased to be the dominant input material but vast quantities of it are still outputted.

We pass now from writing materials to writing implements. The Romans at Vindolanda used a reed pen. In medieval Britain, and indeed for centuries thereafter, there was no serious competition to the quill pen, despite its many shortcomings. The quill pen made the writing of accounts a slow and laborious business. A pen did not last long; the point had constantly to be repaired (with a 'pen' knife) and frequent replenishments with ink were necessary (Whalley, 1975, pp. 19, 41). It was not replaced, however, until the nineteenth century and the quill pen still provides one of the enduring (if misleading) images of accountants.

At last, in the 1830s, mass-produced steel nibs became one of the important products of industrial Birmingham (Whalley, 1975, Chapter 3; Jackson, 1981, Chapter 9). Steel pens still had to be dipped into inkpots at frequent intervals. Fountain pens, which did not, were widely available from the end of the nineteenth century by which time the typewriter was also in general use and the writing of accounts had ceased to become a wholly manual activity (see below). The idea of a ball-point pen also reaches back to the late nineteenth century but the ubiquitous and eponymous biro dates only from

1938 (Jewkes, Sawers and Stillerman, 1969, pp. 234–5; Whalley, 1975, Chapter 9).

NUMERALS

Roman numerals survived even longer in British accounting than the Latin language or parchment. They were, of course, used at Vindolanda. Knowledge of the Arabic (strictly, Hindu-Arabic) numerals reached Western Europe at least as early as the tenth century and their use in business computations was explained in 1202 in the *Liber Abaci* (Book of the Abacus) of Leonardo of Pisa (Smith and Karpinski, 1911). The author of the *Dialogus de Scaccario* (*c.* 1179) was apparently aware of their existence but states that they were not used in the Exchequer (Johnson, 1983, pp. xxxv, 24). The first Scottish and English coins inscribed with Arabic numerals date from 1539 and 1551 respectively (Arbuthnot, 1990, p. 79).

After a comprehensive survey of both public and private records, Jenkinson (1926) came to the following conclusion:

> Arabic numerals do not begin to be at all a common feature in English archives, public or private, before the second quarter of the sixteenth century. Even then their use cannot be called popular or regular save in a very few specific cases: in the vast majority of places where numerals occur the adoption of the Arabic is very slow and sporadic – until the eighteenth century (in some cases even later) the Roman remains an alternative, if not the only form. (p. 264)

It may also be noted that there is no example in England, as there was in Florence in 1299 (Marri, 1955, pp. 72–3; Murray, 1978, pp. 170–1) of guild regulations (in Latin) forbidding the use of Arabic numerals. The lack of such regulations suggests that such numerals were little used.

Jenkinson's conclusion is supported both by the surviving accounts and by the textbooks. Jenkinson (p. 266) found his earliest (*c.* 1490) examples (used only as marginalia) in the Cely papers but there are undoubtedly earlier ones. The account book of Munden's Chantry, Bridport (1453–59), for instance, uses both Arabic and Roman numerals 'indifferently' (Wood-Legh, 1956, p. xxxv).

The most extreme case of conservatism is to be found in the pipe rolls in which Roman numerals were retained until up to the last – 1833! (Galbraith, 1934). Manorial accounts also retain Roman numerals until they ceased to be kept in the sixteenth century. A change from Latin to English was not usually accompanied by the abandonment of Roman numerals. The Hull rentals, for example, were still recorded in Roman numerals in the sixteenth century (Horrox, 1983) despite the change to English in the late fifteenth. The Warden's Accounts of the Worshipful Company of Founders of the City of London 1497–1681 are in English but Roman numerals persisted until 1606 (Parsloe, 1964, pp. 1, 236).

The City of Aberdeen began to adopt Arabic numerals in 1605, the Pewterers Company in 1615, the City of Edinburgh in 1673, and the City of London in 1685 (Boyd, 1905, p. 64). The sixteenth-century accounts of the chamber of the City of London still use mainly Roman numerals (Masters, 1984, p. xLiii).

The accounts of the Corporation of Bristol use Roman numerals until 1640 (apart from two pages in 1635), although from 1586 onwards a note of the total of each page in Arabic figures appears in the left-hand margin (Livock, 1965, p. 88). Other documents published by the Bristol Record Society show Arabic numerals in use for recording monetary amounts, sometimes mixed with Roman, from the beginning of the seventeenth century. Arabic triumphs in mid-century with the last Roman entry in 1661 (Pullan, 1968, pp. 39–41).

Household accounts were usually kept in Roman numerals but there were exceptions. Myers (1985) reproduces four sets from the fifteenth century. The household account of Queen Elizabeth Woodville (wife of Edward IV) for 1466–67 uses Arabic numerals; the others use Roman. The Cromwell household accounts (1417–76) generally use Roman numerals but in one account book Arabic numerals appear occasionally (Myatt-Price, 1956, p. 103). The household accounts of the ninth Earl of Northumberland, 1564–1632, use Roman numerals as do also the Sidney ironworks accounts, 1541–73 (except for the steelworks accounts, 1566), and the accounts of the Roberts family, *c.* 1568–82 (Tittler, 1977–79).

The earliest surviving mercantile accounts – those of William de la Pole and Maghfeld – use Roman numerals. The Celys used both Roman and Arabic in the sixteenth century, but with some apparent preference for the former (Hanham, 1985, p. 165). Halyburton at the turn of the sixteenth century uses mainly Arabic numerals. By this period Arabic numerals in merchants' accounts have still not triumphed completely, however. Of the surviving Tudor account books discussed by Ramsey (1956) – those of Howell, Johnson, Laurence and Gresham – only one (Laurence) uses Arabic throughout. The others display a mixture of Roman and Arabic numerals. Gresham, for example, uses Roman numerals in the money column of his journal but Arabic in the narrative (Littleton and Yamey, 1956, Plate VII). Johnson reverses Gresham's procedure.

Of those sixteenth-century mercantile ledgers not discussed by Ramsey, the ledger of John Smythe (Vanes, 1967, 1974) uses a mixture of Roman and Arabic numerals, although the money columns are usually in Roman. The transition from Roman to Arabic was still taking place in the seventeenth century. The usual practice of John Isham, a late-sixteenth-century mercer and merchant venturer of Northamptonshire, and his clerks was to use Arabic numerals in the narrative of his account books although Arabic and Roman are often jumbled together in the same sentence and even in the same sum of money. Roman numerals were almost always employed in the money columns, except for the totals, which were invariably in Arabic (Ramsey, 1962, p. cxi). David Wedderburne, a merchant of Dundee, in his 'compt buik' (Millar, 1898) extending from 1587 to 1630, uses both notations, as Boyd (1905, p. 64) puts it, 'in the most impartial manner'. Robert Loder's farm accounts (1610–20) were kept mainly in Roman numerals but Arabic were also used (Fussell, 1936, p. xxxi).

What of the evidence of the textbooks, both on arithmetic and book keeping? As late as 1543 (the year of publication of the first English text on double entry) Robert Recorde in his best-selling arithmetic text *The Ground of Artes . . .* refers to 'Arithmetic with the penne' (i.e. with Arabic numerals) and 'the same arte with counters' (i.e. adding with Roman numbers) on terms of equality. A century later the editor of *The Ground of Artes . . .* (1646 edition) refers to ignorant people as 'any that can but cast with counters' (Smith, 1925). Leybourne's *Cursus Mathematicus* (1690) uses Roman numerals to clarify the still not entirely familiar Arabic system (Pullan, 1968, p. 38).

The earliest English language texts on double entry to survive – those by Ympyn (1547), Peele (1553, 1569), Weddington (1567) and Mellis (1588) – show great variety. Ympyn uses Arabic numerals in the narrative but Roman in the money column; Mellis reverses this procedure. Weddington uses Arabic numerals throughout. Peele (1569) in his journal uses Roman numerals in the money column and Arabic in the narrative but the reverse in his ledger. In his book of 1553 he used Arabic numerals in the money columns of both journal and ledger, and Roman numerals in the narratives.

The persistence of Roman numerals in accounting can be most easily explained in terms of costs and benefits. If all that the accountant required was an efficient way of adding up relatively small numbers, Arabic numerals provide few benefits for someone already adept at addition with Roman numerals. Unlike the latter, Arabic numerals do not provide a visual presentation for people who think more in concrete or pictorial terms than in abstracts (Hanham, 1985, p. 165). Thus 'iij' is more plainly one greater than 'ij' than 3 is one greater than 2. Moreover, each Roman numeral corresponded to a counter on the counting board (Pullan, 1986, p. 65). Roman numerals are also more 'natural' in that in counting on one's fingers there is a natural pause at five with a longer break at ten. Whereas Arabic numerals involve successive multiplications of ten, Roman ones break this down into fives and twos. Thus:

Roman		Arabic
I	=	1
V	=	$5 = 5 \times 1$
X	=	$10 = 2 \times 5$
L	=	$50 = 5 \times 10$
C	=	$100 = 2 \times 50$
D	=	$500 = 5 \times 100$
M	=	$1000 = 2 \times 500$

Smith (1925, pp. 90–1) claims that addition with Roman numerals is not difficult and that it is not probable that the accountant was compelled to resort to an abacus when adding, say, 777 to 216. The two systems may be contrasted as follows:

DCCL XX VII	777
CC X VI	216
DCCCCLXXX XIII	993

On the other hand, a possible incentive to move to Arabic notation is that the written figures themselves can be used more conveniently and more effectively in performing actual calculations. The adoption of Arabic numerals meant that the abacus (see below) could be dispensed with, so long as accounting figures were neatly arrayed in columns. Moreover, Arabic numerals have two other advantages: they can be written more concisely than Roman, and they can cope with numbers of unlimited size. In the eighteenth century these advantages became more important as neither Roman numerals nor the counting board could any longer meet the needs of industry and commerce (Pullan, 1968, p. xi).

Smith and Karpinski (1911, p. 136–7) stress the economic importance of writing materials and methods of multiplication and division. Old methods of doing the latter required the erasing of figures after they had served their purpose. It was much cheaper and easier, in the absence of cheap paper (not available until the nineteenth century), to do this by removing counters than by writing and erasing on paper.

Another reason for the persistence of Roman numerals has been advanced by Murray (1978, pp. 169, 198) who suggests a correlation with Latin. Medieval accountants who used Latin were unlikely, he argues, to adopt Arabic numerals because they were 'a suspect novelty from below, unworthy to be allowed among the hallowed customs of literacy'. The evidence does not wholly support this view. As we have already seen, whilst both Latin and Roman numerals persisted in extreme cases until both were abandoned at the same time, in many cases Roman numerals were retained when English replaced Latin.

AIDS TO CALCULATION

The history of calculating aids is often described in terms of a journey 'from the abacus to the computer'. The phrase is misleading if it suggests a smooth progression from a primitive mechanical aid

112

to a very sophisticated one. Rather, four overlapping periods can be discerned:

1. The age of the abacus and counter-casting;
2. The age of 'pen-reckoning' which became dominant in the seventeenth century;
3. The mechanization of the office which began in the nineteenth century; and
4. The age of the computer.

Each calculating aid has its costs and benefits which are a function of:

1. The ease with which the numeral system allows calculation without such aids;
2. The type and frequency of calculations which are required to be made;
3. The costs of acquiring and using the calculating aid.

The first and second of these affects mainly the person keeping the accounts; the third mainly the person for whom they are kept.

Medieval England possessed a numeral system (the Roman) which could benefit more from a calculating aid and was at the same time more adaptable than the Arabic to the line abacus or counting board, whose costs of acquisition and use were remarkably low since all that was required was a flat surface and some counters (Barnard, 1916). Accounting transactions typically involved only the addition of quite small numbers.

The line abacus was probably introduced into England towards the end of the eleventh century (Johnson, 1983, pp. xxxvii). The author of the *Dialogus de Scaccario* (*c.* 1179) describes its operations at the English Exchequer as follows (in Johnson's translation):

> You remember my saying, I imagine, that a cloth is laid on the Exchequer table ruled with lines, and that the coins used as counters are placed in the spaces between them. The Accountant (*calculator*) sits in the middle of his side of the table, so that everybody can see him, and so that his hand can move freely at its work. In the lowest space, on the right, he places the heap of the pence, eleven or fewer. In the second the shillings, up to

nineteen. In the third he puts the pounds . . . In the fourth is the heap of the scores of pounds. In the fifth, hundreds, in the sixth, thousands, in the seventh, but rarely, tens of thousands.

(p. 24)

The merit of the line abacus in its simplest form is that, as shown in Figure 7.1(a), each line and space (which could run horizontally or vertically) represents a distinct Roman numeral. This advantage is lost when (as in the sixteenth-century text referred to below)

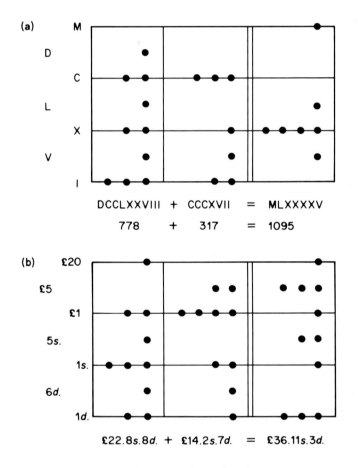

Figure 7.1 Roman v. Arabic numerals on the abacus

114

Arabic numerals are used instead, as is perfectly possible. Alternatively one could ignore the spaces and merely add up in units, tens, hundreds and thousands. This approach, however, produces up to nine counters on a line, whereas most people can only distinguish visually up to five things at a time.

For accounting work the line abacus needed to be adapted, as the quotation from the *Dialogus* shows, to add up in pounds, shillings and pence (12 pence = 1 shilling, 20 shillings = 1 pound). Such an abacus is also illustrated several centuries later in Robert Recorde's *Ground of Artes* (1st edn, 1543, the year of the first English language book on double entry). Here the lines represent one penny, one shilling, one pound, and twenty pounds, and the spaces sixpence, five shillings and five pounds (see Figure 7.1(b)). Recorde uses Arabic numerals instead of Roman but it remains true, as Johnson (1983, p. xxxvi) points out, that the counters in each column were as intelligible to the illiterate as notches on tallies, and the uneducated layman could follow the addition and subtraction (the only mathematical operations needed) as easily as the accountant who recorded his results in Roman numerals. The use of the English Exchequer Table did not finally disappear until 1826 (Pullan, 1968, pp. 2, 121).

The triumph of Arabic numerals over Roman in the seventeenth century did not mean the immediate abandonment of the counting board, as is evidenced by the continued manufacture of counters and by the use of dot diagrams accompanying account totals. These diagrams represented the final position of the counters on the counting board and enabled, for example, Roman numerals to be summed to an Arabic total. By the middle of the eighteenth century few counting boards remained in use and for a long period accountants and merchants used no mechanical aids in their computations and relied entirely on pen-reckoning (Pullan, 1968, Chapter IV).

Machinery did not arrive in the accounts office until the latter half of the nineteenth century. The impetus came from the supply side as technology advanced and from the demands of mathematicians and scientists rather than of accountants. At the same time, the lay user of accounts had become less illiterate and the size of the figures to be added up had increased.

The first commercially successful adding machine in Europe (the 'arithmometer' of Charles Xavier Thomas of Colmar in Alsace) was available from the 1820s, although experimental models had been produced in the seventeenth century in continental Europe by Wilhelm Schickard, Blaise Pascal and Gottfried Leibniz and in England by Sir Samuel Morland. Leibniz's important innovation was the 'stepped reckoner' which allowed multiplication by repeated addition.

From the last quarter of the nineteenth century onwards calculating machines developed in a number of ways with US inventors and manufacturers playing an important role. The main innovations and the most important (not necessarily the first) names associated with them can be summarized as follows (cf. Baxandall and Pugh, 1975):

1. The stepped reckoner was replaced by a wheel having a variable number of projecting fingers, or teeth (F.S. Baldwin, 1875; W.T. Ohdner, 1891). The machine was operated manually by a handle.
2. A keyboard was added. These types of machines were of two types being operated either by –
   (a) depressing the figure keys; or by
   (b) depressing a handle after the figure keys had been set.
   Type (a) was marketed as the very successful 'comptometer' (Dorr E. Felt, 1887).
3. A print-out was added, i.e. the calculator became an adding listing machine (W.S. Burroughs, 1892).
4. Multiplication and division were performed directly (L. Bollée, 1887).
5. Electric motors were added (*c.* 1900).
6. The calculator was combined with the typewriter in an accounting machine which not only added and listed but produced a horizontal record of each accounting transaction (1920s) (see Morgan, 1953).
7. The number of keys for numerals was reduced to ten (1950s).
8. The electronic calculator was introduced (the Anita, 1961).

The early 1970s saw the advent of the pocket calculator and the programmable calculator.

The spread of mechanical aids of calculation in British professional offices was held back by the cheapness of clerical labour and the custom until the 1950s of not paying articled clerks. Kohler (1987, p. 24) recalls that in the firm in which he trained in the early 1930s articled clerks and audit clerks still did most of the routine arithmetic by hand on sheets of paper. The firm was unwilling to spend a lot of money on what it regarded as a 'newfangled gadget' when the time taken by manual calculation was free.

Clerical labour had been scarcer during the First World War. It was in the middle of this war that Dicksee, lecturing to the Chartered Accountant Students Society of London, claimed that the choice lay between doing work with the aid of machinery or leaving it undone. Describing comptometers, Burroughs adding machines and other readily available office machinery he urged that: 'All that is required is that we should overcome our prejudice against using it, and turn our attention to the consideration of the problem as to how it may be used most extensively and to the best advantage' (Dicksee, 1916, p. 666).

In this and other lectures Dicksee's writings take on a missionary flavour. He was opposing a general unwillingness to change, not just rational decisions to prefer cheap labour to expensive machinery. He was, of course, aware of the latter argument. His 1916 lecture also contained a description of Hollerith machines and he pointed out that the cost of an installation was only £150 p.a., equal to the 'salary paid to an ordinary experienced clerk' (p. 666).

Hollerith machines were, before the advent of the computer, the most advanced form of mechanical aid to calculation. These electro-mechanical punched card calculating machines had been invented in the late 1880s by Herman Hollerith, a statistician on the staff of the US Bureau of the Census. Punched card machines were used to analyse the results of the US census of 1890 and first applied to a UK census in 1911. In his 1916 lecture Dicksee referred to two installations he had personally inspected – those of the Gas Department of the Birmingham Corporation and the British Westinghouse Company. A punched card installation typically consisted of a hand punch, a verifier, a sorter, a reproducer, a tabulator and a collator. Punched card installations became relatively common from the 1920s but were eventually superseded by electronic computers. The first generation of computers appeared in both the UK and the USA in 1943. Their forerunners (which had no influence on accounting at the time) were the difference engine (1821) and the analytical engine (never completed) of Charles Babbage (1792–1871) and his co-worker Ada Lovelace. Babbage understood the essential elements of any computing system, namely input (for which he, as Hollerith was to do later, used the punched cards originally developed by Jacquard in 1801 for the automatic control of textile looms); store (for which he considered the use of punched cards and metal disks on spindles); processing unit; and output (for which he considered using punched cards and automatic typesetting).

The first British computer was Colossus I, a special-purpose machine built in 1943 to decipher the messages produced by Enigma, the German code generator. The earliest commercial application came in 1951 when the cost accounting analysis of Cadby Hall Bakeries (part of J. Lyons & Co. Ltd) was performed by LEO (Lyons Electronic Office), based on the scientific computer EDSAC (Electronic Delay Storage Automatic Computer), built at Cambridge University in 1949.

By the later 1950s, accounting calculations, especially those relating to payroll and stock control, had overtaken scientific and technical calculations as the most common use of computers. The first generation of computers (1943–55), built out of thermionic valves, virtually ignored input–output equipment. With the second, transistorized, generation (1956–63) and the growth of commercial applications, input and output became much more important. Paper tape and magnetic tape were used as well as punched cards. Output was mainly sheets of continuous paper stationery. Accounting relied more than ever on paper as a 'writing' material.

The third (1964–81) and fourth (1982–) generations of computers introduced minicomputers and microcomputers. By 1988, computers had ceased to input paper but were outputting it in larger and larger quantities – perhaps because office automation has simply meant 'transferring inefficient and inappropriate paperbased systems onto computers' (Bentley, 1988, p. 14).

The use of computers for the keeping of accounting records was first recognized in British legislation by The Stock Exchange (Completion of Bargains) Act 1976, s. 3 (now s. 723, Companies Act 1985). The section allows the use of computers so long as the recording is capable of being reproduced in a legible form. The law does not state that the records must be reproduced in such a form or that the output must be on paper.

SUMMARY AND CONCLUSIONS

Language, writing materials, numerals and calculation are essential to all but the most primitive forms of accounting. This paper has traced their development in British accounting and shown how choices had to be made between English, French and Latin; wood, parchment and paper; Roman and Arabic numerals; and counting boards, pen reckoning, electromechanical calculators amd computers.

No attempt has been made to look at other countries. The experience of those in continental Europe might be expected not to differ too much, except chronologically, from Britain's. The Gallerani company of Siena, whose London branch accounts (1305–08) have already been referred to, can be used as an example. The accounts were kept in Italian, in a paper book, using a mixture of Roman and Arabic numerals. The accounts of the Paris branch, which have also survived, were kept in Italian, in a *parchment* book, in a mixture of Roman and Arabic (Bigwood and Grunzweig, 1962, pp. 9, 13–4). Newer countries such as the USA and Australia have had simpler histories, Countries such as Nigeria and Malaysia are interesting in that English fulfils much the same role as Latin once did in Britain.

The evidence collected in this paper provides some support, it is suggested, for the hypothesis that the choices made of language, materials, numerals and calculating aids have depended upon assessments of costs and benefits made both by those who kept the accounts and those for whom they were kept and with attention paid to the needs of external users.

(The author is grateful for the detailed comments of C. W. Nobes on a previous draft of this paper.)

REFERENCES

Arbuthnot, R.F. (1900) *The Mysteries of Chronology*, Heinemann, London.
Baker, J.H. (1979) *Manual of Law French*, Avebury.

Barber, C. (1976) *Early Modern English,* André Deutsch, London.

Barnard, F.P. (1916) *The Casting Counter and the Counting Board,* Clarendon Press, Oxford; reprinted (1981) Fox Publications, Yeovil.

Batho, G.R. (ed.) (1962) *The Household Papers of Henry Percy. Ninth Earl of Northumberland (1564–1632),* Camden Third Series, volume 93.

Baugh, A.C. (1957) *A History of the English Language,* 2nd edition, Appleton-Century-Crofts, New York.

Baxandall, D. and Pugh, J. (1975) *Calculating Machines and Instruments,* revised edition, Science Museum, London.

Bentley, T. (1988) Office automation – triggering the paperwork explosion, *Management Accounting,* May.

Bigwood, G. and Grunzweig, A. (1962) *Les Livres des Comptes des Gallerani,* volume 2, Académie Royale de Belgique, Brussels.

Bowman, A.K. (1983) *The Roman Writing Tablets from Vindolanda,* British Museum Publications, London.

Bowman, A.K. and Thomas, J.D. (1983) *Vindolanda: The Latin Writing Tablets,* Alan Sutton, London.

Boyd, E. (1905) Early forms of accounts, in *A History of Accounting and Accountants,* R. Brown (ed.), Jack, Edinburgh.

Clanchy, M.T. (1979) *From Memory to Written Record: England 1066–1307,* Edward Arnold, London.

Coleman, D.C. (1958) *The British Paper Industry 1495–1860,* Clarendon Press, Oxford.

Connell-Smith, G.E. (1950) Ledger of Thomas Howell, *Economic History Review,* second series, volume 3.

Croix, G.E.M. de Ste (1956) Greek and Roman accounting, in Littleton and Yamey.

Crossley. D.W. (1975) *Sydney Ironworks Accounts 1541–1573,* volume 15, Camden Fourth Series, London.

Delgado, A. (1979) *The Enormous File,* John Murray, London.

Dhondt, J. (1964) *Finance et comptabilité urbaines du XIIIe au XVIe siècle,* volume VII, 8th series, Pro Civitate, Brussels.

Dicksee, L.R. (1911) *Advanced Accounting,* 4th edition, Gee & Co., London.

Dicksee, L.R. (1916) Machinery as an aid to accountancy, *Accountant,* 10 June.

Diringer D. (1953) *The Hand-Produced Book,* Hutchinson, London.

Fielding, K.J. (1960) *The Speeches of Charles Dickens,* Clarendon Press, Oxford.

Fryde, E.B. (1964) *The Wool Accounts of William de la Pole,* St Anthony's Press, York; reprinted in Fryde, E. B. (1982) *Studies in Medieval Trade and Finance,* Hambledon Press, London.

Fussell, G.E. (ed.) (1936) *Robert Loder's Farm Accounts 1610–1620*, volume LIII, Camden Third Series, London.

Galbraith. V.H. (1934) *An Introduction to the Use of the Public Records*, Oxford University Press, London.

Gaur, A. (1987) *A History of Writing*, 2nd edition, The British Library, London.

Hanham, A. (1985) *The Celys and Their World*, Cambridge University Press, Cambridge.

Harrison, F. (1943) *A Book About Books*, John Murray, London.

Harvey, P.D.A. (1984) *Manorial Records*, British Records Association, London.

Hills, R. (1988) The history of papermaking in the UK: Part 1, *Paper Focus*, February.

Horrox, R. (ed.) (1983) *Selected Rentals and Accounts of Medieval Hull, 1293–1528*, volume CXLI, The Yorkshire Archaeological Society Record Series, Leeds.

Hunter, D. (1947) *Papermaking: The History and Technique of an Ancient Craft*, 2nd edition, Dover Publications, New York.

Innes, C. (ed.) (1867) *Ledger of Andrew Halyburton, 1492–1503*, Her Majesty's General Register House, Edinburgh.

Jackson, D. (1981) *The Story of Writing*, Barrie & Jenkins, London.

James, M.E. (ed.) (1955) *Estate Accounts of the Earls of Northumberland 1562–1637*, volume CLXIII, Publications of the Surtees Society.

Jenkins, R. (1900) Early attempts at paper-making in England, 1495–1586, *Library Association Record*, September.

Jenkinson, H. (1911) Exchequer tallies, *Archaeologia*, LXII.

Jenkinson, H. (1925) Medieval tallies, public and private, *Archaeologia*, LXXIV.

Jenkinson, H. (1926) The use of Arabic and Roman numerals in English archives, *Antiquaries Journal*, July.

Jewkes, J. Sawers, D. and Stillerman, R. (1969) *The Sources of Invention*, 2nd edition, Macmillan, London.

Johnson, C. (1925) Introduction to Stenton, D.M. (ed.) *The Great Roll of the Pipe for the Second Year of the Reign of King Richard the First*, Publications of the Pipe Roll Society, volume 39, NS, volume 1, London.

Johnson, C. (1983) *Dialogus de Scaccario* . . . Clarendon Press. Oxford.

K[ats], P. (1926). Double entry book-keeping in England before Hugh Oldcastle, *Accountant*, LXXIV.

Kingsford, C.L. (1925) *Prejudice and Promise in Fifteenth Century England*, London. Reprinted: 1962, Frank Cass. London.

Kohler. C. (1987), *Five Years Hard! Memoirs of an Articled Clerk 1928–1933*, Chartac Books, London.

Lapsley. C.T. (1899). Account rolls of a fifteenth century ironmaster, *English Historical Review*, 14.

Littleton, A.C. (1946). The horizontal ledger and early accounting machines, *Accounting Review*.

Littleton, A.C. and Yamey, B.S. (1956), *Studies in the History of Accounting*, Sweet and Maxwell, London.

Livock, D.M. (1965). The accounts of the Corporation of Bristol, 1532 to 1835. *Journal of Accounting Research*, 3.

Marri, G.C. (1955), *Statuti dell'Arte del Cambio di Firenze, 1299–1316*, Florence.

Masters, B.R. (1984) *Chambers Accounts of the Sixteenth Century*, London Record Society Publications, London.

Millar, A.H. (1898), *The Compt Buik of David Wedderburne Merchant of Dundee 1587–1630* . . . Publications of the Scottish History Society, Edinburgh volume xxxviii.

Morgan, B. (1953), *Total to Date. The Evolution of the Adding Machine: The Story of Borroughs*, Burroughs Adding Machine Ltd, London.

Murray, A. (1978), *Reason and Society in the Middle Ages*, Clarendon Press, Oxford.

Myatt-Price, E.M. (1956), Cromwell household accounts, 1417–1476. In Littleton and Yamey.

Myers, A.R. (1985), *Crown, Household and Parliament in Fifteenth Century England*, (ed. C.H. Clough), The Hambledon Press. London.

Nobes, C.W. (1982), The Gallerani account book of 1305–1308, *Accounting Review*.

North, R. (1714), *The Gentleman Accomptant*, E. Curll, London; reprinted 1986, Garland Publishing, New York.

Oschinsky, D. (1971), *Walter of Henley and Other Treatises on Estate Management and Accounting*, Clarendon Press, Oxford.

Parker, R.H. (1984a). Reckoning, merchants' accounts, book keeping, accounting or accountancy? The evidence of the long titles of books on accounting in English, 1543–1914. In *External Financial Reporting* (eds B. Carsberg and S. Dev), Prentice-Hall International, London.

Parker, R.H. (1984b), Burning down Parliament: A story of accounting change, *Accountancy*, October.

Parsloe, G. (1974), *Warden's Accounts of the Worshipful Company of Founders of the City of London 1467–1681*, The Athlone Press, London.

Plant, M. (1974) *The English Book Trade*, 3rd edition, George Allen & Unwin. London.

Price, G. (1984) *The Languages of Britain*, Edward Arnold, London.

Pullan, J.M. (1968), *The History of the Abacus*, Hutchinson, London.

Ramsay, G.D. (ed.) (1962) *John Isham Mercer and Merchant Adventurer: Two Account Books of a London Merchant in the Reign of Elizabeth I*, volume XXI, Publications of the Northamptonshire Record Society, Gateshead.

Ramsey, P. (1956) Some Tudor merchants' accounts. In Littleton and Yamey.

Reed, R. (1972) *Ancient Skins, Parchments and Leathers*, Seminar Press, London.

Richardson, H.G. (1941) Business training in medieval Oxford, *American Historical Review*, XLVI.

Rickert, E. (1926–27) Extracts from a fourteenth-century account book, *Modern Philology*, XXIV.

Ritson, F.A. (1966) Halyburton's ledger and his times, *Accountants' Magazine*, LXX.

Roberts, C.R. and Skeat, T.C. (1983) *The Birth of the Codex*, Oxford University Press for the British Academy, London.

Smith, D.E. (1925), *History of Mathematics*, volume 2, Ginn & Co., New York.

Smith, D.E. and Karpinski, L.C. (1911) *The Hindu-Arabic Numerals*, Ginn & Co., Boston.

Sorter, G.H. (1969) An 'events' approach to basic accounting theory, *Accounting Review*.

Stoeckel, H.J. (1946) Loose-leaf and accounting, *Accounting Review*.

Tittler, R. (ed.) (1977–79) *Accounts of the Roberts Family of Boarzell, Sussex c. 1568–1582*. volume 71, Sussex Record Society.

Vanes, J. (1967) The ledger of John Smythe, merchant of Bristol, *Accountant*, September 16.

Vanes, J. (ed.) (1974) *The Ledger of John Smythe, 1438–1550*, Royal Commission on Historical Manuscripts, JP 19, HMSO, London.

Walker, D. (1980) Language, legal, in Walker, D. *The Oxford Companion to Law*, Clarendon Press, Oxford.

Whalley, J.I. (1975) *Writing Implements and Accessories*, David & Charles, Newton Abbot.

Whalley, J.I. (1980) *The Universal Penman*, HMSO, London.

Wood-Legh, K.L. (ed.) (1956) *A Small Household of the XVth Century, Being the Account Book of Munden's Chantry, Bridport*, Manchester University Press, Manchester.

Yamey, B.S. (1961) The word 'ledger', *Accountancy*, March.

8

The true and fair view doctrine: some recent developments

B.A. RUTHERFORD

Peter Bird's attitude to the true and fair view was characteristic of him, both as an individual and as a scholar: his willingness to work with the grain of professional thinking made him prepared to assume that the phrase had a meaning; his intellectual honesty forced him to concede that this assumption might be false. The following quotation reflects his position very well. Discussing the famous *Argyll* case and the subsequent Statement from the Department of Trade, he wrote:

> . . . neither the case itself nor subsequent consideration and the Department's statement cast much light on the meaning of 'a true and fair view'. But we have obtained important clarification of the relationship between the true and fair view (assuming that we recognize one when we find one), the other requirements of the Companies Acts and professional Statements of Standard Accounting Practice.
>
> (Bird 1982, pp. 364–5)

This paper examines some recent developments affecting the true and fair view (henceforth TFV) doctrine and the arguments for and against its use.

TFV IN AUSTRIALIA

At first sight the requirement in the Australian Companies Act and Code 1984 that financial statements show a TFV appears identical to that of British law. There is, however, at least one important difference. While the legislation provides that:

> where accounts . . . prepared in accordance with [the Act's detailed] requirements would not otherwise give a true and fair view of the matters required . . . to be dealt with in the accounts . . . the directors of the company shall *add* such information and explanations as will give a true and fair view of those matters,
>
> (s. 269(8), emphasis added.)

there is no equivalent to the British provision that a company must *depart from* the detailed requirements of the legislation if compliance will not yield a TFV and additional disclosure cannot by itself remedy the position (Companies Act 1985, s. 228(5) – see Kenley (1984).)

How can the absence of the 'departure provision' be explained? It would appear that either the detailed requirements of the Australian legislation have been framed in such a way that they cannot conflict with TFV or that the Australian TFV is somehow constrained while, at least for Australians, remaining true and fair. A scrutiny of the detailed requirements reveals nothing particularly unusual by comparison with the British position so that the latter explanation seems more likely; the much-vaunted capacity of TFV to cope with new and unusual situations must thus be somewhat undermined in Australia.

The TFV provisions of the Australian legislation were the subject of a highly controversial 'green paper' written by Bob Walker, Professor of Accountancy at the University of New South Wales, and issued by the National Companies and Securities Commission in 1984. Walker suggested that the Companies Act be amended to read:

> Without affecting the generality of the meaning of the term 'true and fair view', a 'true and fair view' in relation to accounts or group accounts means a representation which

affords those who might reasonably be expected to refer to those accounts (including holders or prospective purchasers of shares, debentures, notes or other interests, and creditors or prospective creditors) information which is relevant to the decisions which may be made by those persons in relation to the purchase, sale or other action in connection with their securities or interests.

(para. 7.6)

The profession reacted to this proposal with undisguised horror. In a joint submission to the National Companies and Securities Commission, the Australian Society of Accountants and the Institute of Chartered Accountants in Australia (1985) said:

[We] do not see how the wording Professor Walker proposes to be added to the definitions enumerated in . . . the Act will:
(a) clarify the meaning of a 'true and fair view' in relation to financial reporting;
(b) properly or effectively identify the groups intended to be served by financial reporting; and [*sic*]
(c) make more enforceable any action arising from non-compliance with the requirement to give a 'true and fair view'.

In our view the suggested amendment will only serve to create greater uncertainty by introducing the proposition that accounts should contain 'information which is relevant' to an undefined (seemingly all inclusive) group of users for an undefined (but seemingly all inclusive) range of purposes. The proposition is not feasible and would place an impossible responsibility on auditors (and directors).

(para. 30)

Instead the accountancy bodies rejected any attempt to, as they put it, 'patch' TFV and advocated a requirement that the financial statements should:

Present fairly the financial position . . . and profit (or loss) . . . in accordance with approved accounting standards and comply with the Companies Code.

(para. 2)

Although few commentators go as far as Walker, many hint that what constitutes a TFV might (or should) be connected in some way with user needs. Flint (1982), for example, argues that:

> The annual accounts are important as a prime source of information on which investment decisions are taken and on which the value of securities is agreed between buyers and sellers. The view which is given of profit or loss and state of affairs, to the extent that this can be given in annual accounts, must be true and fair in relation to the interests of these parties. This means not only that the information has to be adequate for the needs of any one party but also that it has to be even-handed as between parties.
>
> (p. 25)

Again, for Tweedie (1983), 'truth and fairness . . . have to be related to the purposes for which the accounts have been prepared' (p. 426). The reaction of the Australian accountancy bodies to the NCSC green paper and their proposal actually to abandon TFV, however, suggest that user-need based interpretations of TFV are unlikely to prove popular with the profession at large.

TFV IN THE EC

The UK has exported TFV to the rest of the EC by means of the Fourth Company Law Directive. The first draft of the directive was issued prior to the UK's accession to the EC and required that accounts 'conform to the principles of regular and proper accounting' (Tweedie, 1983). It is well known that it was British influence, after the entry of the UK, that resulted in the requirement being redrafted along TFV lines. The wording of the directive makes it clear that TFV is an overriding requirement and that companies must depart from the specific requirements of legislation if it is necessary in order to achieve TFV. Despite this:

> Germany has not included a provision in its law that a company must depart from the requirements of the law in order to give a true and fair view, nor does the present law in Portugal [sic]. Italy's law states that a company 'may depart'.

... Germany has included a provision in its law that, if special circumstances result in the financial statements not showing a true and fair view, then additional disclosures are required in the notes to the accounts.

(Commission of the European Communities 1987, p. 5.)

The French version of the Fourth Directive requires that financial statements give 'une image fidèle' ('a faithful image'). On being told that TFV was not defined in British law because the British knew a TFV when they saw one, the French representatives are claimed to have replied, 'c'est comme l'amour' (see Rutteman (1987)); in print they have been more circumspect, describing 'une image fidèle' as:

[Une] *mauvaise* traduction de la 'true and fair view' des Anglo-Saxons qui n'ont pas cherché à définir ce concept. [A bad translation of the 'true and fair view' of the Anglo-Saxons who have not sought to define the concept.]

(CNCC, 1984, p. I.4, emphasis supplied.)

The TFV appears to have been adopted in the 1986 *Plan Comptable Général* which requires that:

A l'effet de présenter des états reflétant une image fidèle de la situation et des opérations de l'enterprise, la comptabilité doit satisfaire, dans le respect de la règle de prudence, aux obligations de régularité et de sincérité. [In order to present financial statements reflecting a true and fair view of the state of the enterprise, financial accounting must satisfy, in respect of the principle of prudence, the requirements of regularity and sincerity.] (p. I.5)

'Regularity' implies compliance with the regulations while 'sincerity' involves the application of 'bonne foi' ('good faith') in such compliance. The requirement *before* the implementation of the Fourth Directive, when the French were apparently untouched by TFV, was that auditors certify as to the 'regularity and sincerity' of the accounts (Pham, 1984). The phrase which springs to mind is 'plus ça change, plus c'est la même chose'.

It is sometimes suggested that the Germans' refusal to allow TFV to override the detailed regulations is attributable to a belief that, provided such regulations are drafted with sufficient care, they could never result in a view that was not true and fair. Hence an override is unnecessary (Rutteman, 1987). However, the inclusion in their legislation of a requirement for additional disclosure where special circumstances result in the financial statements not showing a TFV suggests that this belief is not absolute. None the less the effect of the German drafting is that it is not possible to depart from the detailed regulations on the basis of a TFV override.

TFV IN HONG KONG

The legal regime in Hong Kong offers the intriguing possibility of comparing different overriding criteria. The Hong Kong Companies Ordinance contains a requirement that financial statements should show a TFV; however, in the case of exempt private companies, the requirement is that the financial statements show a true and *correct* view. This was, of course, also the general test in British company law from 1900 until its displacement by TFV in the 1947 Companies Act (Rutherford, 1985). In proposing the change The Institute of Chartered Accountants in England and Wales argued that 'some people feel that in dealing with matters of estimate . . . the word "correct" is rather too rigid' (Rutherford, 1985). In view of this it is perhaps surprising that in Hong Kong:

> Smaller practitioners, most of whom carry out substantial numbers of 'true and correct' audits, often charge lower audit fees and consequently [*sic*] carry out much less extensive testing on such companies.
>
> (*World Accounting Report*, 1986, p. 20.)

Although less extensive testing might be an appropriate response to an organization being an exempt private company it is difficult to see how it could spring from the use of the term 'correct' rather than 'fair'.

Put to it to identify the real difference between true and correct and true and fair, the Hong Kong Society of Accountants 'admitted that there is no clear legal distinction' and 'acting on legal advice . . . recommended that auditors ignore the differences in the reporting requirements' (*World Accounting Report*, 1986, p. 20). This surely creates difficulties for those who would seek to interpret TFV by a close scrutiny of the particular words used (see Rutherford, 1985).

TFV AND INTERNATIONAL AUDITING GUIDELINES

International Auditing Guideline 13, *The Auditor's Report on Financial Statements*, which was issued in 1983, refers to TFV but in a manner quite alien to British practice:

> The [auditor's] report should clearly set forth the auditor's opinion on the presentation in the financial statements of the entity's financial position and the results of its operations. The words suggested to express the auditor's opinion are 'give a true and fair view (or 'present fairly') . . . in accordance with [indicate relevant national standards or International Accounting Standards]'.
>
> (paras 8 and 9; first square brackets added, ellipsis and second square brackets in original text.)

This form of words links TFV to compliance with GAAP rather than representing an overriding criterion; apparently the approach adopted in the standard was opposed only by the UK and Ireland (Tweedie, 1983).

TFV AND DEFICIENCIES IN GAAP

One difficulty that those who make optimistic claims about the efficacy of the TFV doctrine face is that in practice financial statements which appear to fall short of what is implied by these claims, yet which comply with generally accepted accounting principles, do not attract audit qualifications or prosecution. Flint (1982), for example, believes that the TFV doctrine provides 'a safety valve protecting users from bias, inadequacy or deficiency in the rules' and 'an enduring conceptual standard for disclosure in accounting and reporting to ensure that there is always relevant disclosure' (p. 30). Yet, in discussing TFV in the context of consolidated accounting within the EC, Flint (1988) himself explains that:

. . . Difficult questions arise with the absence of consensus in accounting thought on matters such as the alternative methods of consolidation, the valuation of non-cash consideration, the fair value of the net assets of a subsidiary, the appropriate treatment of minority interests, valuation and treatment of goodwill on consolidation, translation of foreign currency and the effect of price level changes (particularly with differential rates of inflation coupled with changing relative currency values). (p. 33)

Although he appears to suggest that 'free choice' of accounting policy in all these areas can be justified on the basis that all produce *a* TFV, though not the same one, he goes on to argue that:

The fact is that the requirement to give 'a true and fair view' should make it impossible for these variations to survive . . .
(p. 34)

The fact is, surely, that most of the variations catalogued by Flint have been in existence within the UK for the forty or so years that consolidated accounts have been required to show a TFV and that few financial statements have attracted qualification or prosecution as a result. In so far as the number of variants of policy available in consolidated accounts is declining there is no evidence that it is as a result of the requirement to show a TFV.

Flint appears also to be rather embarrassed by the persistence of historical cost accounting through periods of high inflation. Writing in 1984, he argued that:

Although the [1981 Companies] Act is silent on the matter, the question which must be addressed is whether, on any reasonable interpretation of a true and fair view of the state of affairs or of the profit or loss of a company, amounts included in accounts, determined in accordance with the historical cost accounting rules, could on their own, without additions and/or departures, be able to give that view.
(p. 104)

He went on to explain that although a then current SSAP dealt with current cost accounting, the accounting profession did not require that historical cost financial statements unaccompanied by current cost information should, merely because of that omission, be qualified as failing to provide a TFV:

> It appears, therefore, that the opinion which is expressed above on the interpretation of a 'true and fair view' in current economic conditions is not one which is held by the Councils of the professional accountancy bodies.
>
> (p. 108)

As Flint points out it is in principle possible that, asked to adjudicate on the matter, the courts would rule that current cost information was essential to a TFV so that the many thousands of sets of financial statements issued during the high inflation of the 1970s and early 1980s without such information (and their accompanying audit reports) would have been in breach of the law. None the less, in practice the courts were not asked to rule on the question so that the existence of a requirement to show a TFV failed to achieve a reform which Flint apparently regarded as desirable if not essential.

This section is not an attack on Flint's views on the deficiencies of GAAP; indeed the present author largely shares those views. Rather, the point is to suggest that, in the face of the continuing failure of TFV in the UK to repair what Flint (and others) perceive as deficiencies in GAAP, their support for TFV – given on the basis of its capacity to overcome such deficiencies – must surely be provisional.

'TRUE' AND 'FAIR' OR 'TRUE AND FAIR'

The controversy between those for whom TFV is a single test and those who see it as imposing two separate tests continues. In Lee's view (1982):

> It is difficult to conceive of how company directors, auditors and report users are to interpret it as a single concept when it is plain that it is worded as truth *and* fairness. (p. 18)

For Davison (1983), however:

> The true and fair view is . . . a hyphenated phrase which loses

133

its essential meaning if the words are considered separately. . . . Sadly, few judges seem to have grasped this point . . .

(p. 3)

Incidentally, the many commentators for whom TFV is 'a jurisprudential concept' (Flint, 1984) so that:

the answers to the questions which have been posed about its interpretation in specific terms are dependent on the view which would be taken by the Courts . . .　　　　(p. 109)

would presumably dissent from Davison's robust view that the judiciary cannot be relied upon to grasp the essence of the doctrine.

TFV OF WHAT?

Discussion of the TFV doctrine sometimes overlooks the words surrounding the bare phrase 'true and fair'. In the British legislation the requirement is that:

The balance sheet shall give a true and fair view of the state of affairs of the company as at the end of the financial year; and the profit and loss account shall give a true and fair view of the profit or loss of the company for the financial year.

(s. 228(2), Companies Act 1985)

Even friends of TFV sometimes have qualms about the other words in the requirement:

It is clearly necessary to consider what is meant by 'the state of affairs' of a company. The EEC Fourth Directive on Company Law [see above] requires that the annual accounts shall give a true and fair view of the company's assets, liabilities, financial position and profit or loss. . . . While 'state of affairs' may not be wholly synonymous with 'financial position' [strictly, presumably, 'assets, liabilities' and 'financial position'] it must certainly, at least, include it. The expression 'state of affairs' is long established in Great Britain but it has not been the subject of statutory or judicial interpretation. It must be asked whether its meaning and the meaning of 'financial position' are singular and obvious.

(Flint, 1984, pp. 103–4.)

There is surely a certain irony in a supporter of TFV (see above) complaining that the phrase 'state of affairs' lacks statutory or judicial interpretation.

THE EXTENSION OF TFV BEYOND COMPANY FINANCIAL STATEMENTS

The profession regularly advocates the extension of the TFV doctrine to financial statements beyond those of companies and, indeed, uses the term in such cases (Rutherford, 1985, pp. 484–5). An interesting recent case of the adoption of TFV relates to tax relief for profit-related pay. Schemes to obtain such relief must provide for the preparation of a profit and loss account for each 'employment unit':

> Where the employment unit is a sub-unit of the business, it will be necessary to include in the profit and loss account figures relating to transactions between the sub-unit and the rest of the business. A formal invoicing system to support those figures is not essential, but the independent accountant . . . must still be able to sign a report that the profit or loss is a 'true and fair' one.
>
> (Inland Revenue 1987, para 6.55.)

This requirement extends TFV both to non-company enterprises (such as partnerships), which are entitled to operate profit-related pay schemes, and to sub-units within companies. The use of TFV here appears to raise a number of problems. To whom will the report be issued? How will a report qualified, either on the basis of a qualification in the company financial statements or because of some consideration applying at the sub-unit level, be treated? Employees might be concerned, for example, to discover that a debit adjustment to profit which had been ignored in the company's financial statements became material, and hence required to be made, in the statements used to calculate their tax-relieved pay. Both statements could receive an unqualified TFV opinion and, while this would be unlikely to be the point uppermost in employees' minds, the credibility of TFV could only be reduced.

Perhaps the most serious problem is whether the level of inter-sub-unit transactions could undermine the scope for providing an unqualified TFV opinion. Certainly if this is not the case the argument against segmented reporting on the grounds that inter-segment transactions limit the objectivity of the report would appear to fall.

Keen TFV-watchers take as much interest in financial reporting regimes which fail to employ TFV as in those that do and in this context the preference in the new Code of Practice on Local Authority Accounting (CIPFA, 1987) for 'present fairly' may be significant. The relevant section of the Code requires that:

> A statement of accounts shall present fairly the financial position and transactions of the authority. 'Fair presentation' will normally be achieved by compliance in all material respects with proper local authority accounting practices and in particular with this Accounting Code of Practice as regards form and content, and the broad accounting concepts outlined [in the Code]. Where the requirements of the Code are not met, then full disclosure and, where relevant, quantification of the departure in the statement of accounts is required.
>
> (para. 3.2)

The use of 'normally', however, implies that it is possible to depart from the Code (provided that the departure is disclosed and, where relevant, quantified) in pursuit of fair presentation, so that the Code's requirement is not equivalent to a 'presents fairly in accordance with' requirement, as advocated by the Australian accountancy bodies (see above).

CONCLUSION

The TFV doctrine has been exported to the rest of the EC 'successfully' in the sense that it was accepted into the Fourth Directive and no member state has explicitly refused to implement that Directive. It is difficult not to feel, however, that the manner of its implementation has subverted whatever meaning its advocates presumably believe that it has. Perhaps the apparent ease of this subversion is attributable to the doctrine's lack of substance.

The continuing absence of judicial interpretation provides ambiguous evidence of the efficacy of TFV: can it be that cases do not get to court because all accountants instinctively recognize a TFV and thus have no need for judicial interpretation? The alternative, of course, is that the term is so ambiguous that no potential litigant could have rational grounds for supposing that he or she would win a case.

The trend internationally, as evidenced by developments in Australia and IFAC, suggests that support for an overriding TFV is weak and weakening. Whether the British profession will wish to follow this trend is another matter; if not, it is surely time for it to address itself explicitly and authoritatively to the question of what framework of principles could be used to justify departure from GAAP in pursuit of a TFV.

REFERENCES

Australian Society of Accountants and Institute of Chartered Accountants in Australia (1985) Submission to the National Companies and Securities Commission on the Consultative Document, '*A True and Fair View' and the Reporting Obligations of Directors and Auditors*, ASA and ICAA, Melbourne and Sydney.

Bird, P.A. (1982) Group accounts and the true and fair view, *The Journal of Business Law*, 364–8.

Chartered Institute of Public Finance and Accountancy (1987) *Code of Practice on Local Authority Accounting*, CIPFA, London.

Commission of the European Communities (1987) Document: *The Fourth Company Law Directive: Implementation by Member States* (CB-48-87-484-EN-C), Office for Official Publications of the European Communities, Luxemburg.

Compagnie Nationale des Commissaires aux Comptes (1984) *Assises Nationales du Commissariat aux Comptes* (Documents de travail), CNCC, Paris.

Davison, I.H. (1983) *Accounting Standards: The True and Fair View and the Law*, Arthur Andersen & Co., London.

Flint, D. (1982) *A True and Fair View in Company Accounts*, Gee & Co. for the Institute of Chartered Accountants of Scotland, London.

Flint, D. (1984) A true and fair view: a UK perspective, in *EEC Accounting Harmonization: Implementation and Impact of the Fourth Directive*, S.J. Gray and A. G. Coenenberg (eds), North-Holland, Amsterdam.

Flint, D. (1988) A true and fair view in consolidated accounts, in

International Group Accounting, S.J. Gray and A.G. Coenenberg (eds), Croom Helm, London.

Inland Revenue (1987) *Tax Relief for Profit-Related Pay: Notes for Guidance* (PRP 2), Inland Revenue, London.

Kenley, J. (1984) True and fair rules – some Australian observations, *The Accountant's Magazine*, March, 88: 933, 98–9.

Lee, T.A. (1982) The will-o'-the-wisp of 'true and fair', *The Accountant*, 15 July, 187 : 5601, 96–8.

National Companies and Securities Commission [Australia] (1984) '*A True and Fair View' and the Reporting Obligations of Directors and Auditors: A Consultative Document with Proposals for Reform of Provisions of the Companies Act and Code*, NCSC, Melbourne.

Pham, D. (1984) A true and fair view: a French perspective, in *EEC Accounting Harmonization: Implementation and Impact of the Fourth Directive*, S.J. Gray and A.G. Coenenberg (eds), North-Holland, Amsterdam.

Rutherford, B.A. (1985) The true and fair view doctrine: a search for explication, *Journal of Business Finance and Accounting*, 12 : 4, 483–94.

Rutteman, P. (1987) *Accounting Standards in Europe: The Way Ahead*, Plenary paper presented at the Tenth Annual Congress of the European Accounting Association.

Tweedie, D. (1983) True and fair rules, *The Accountant's Magazine*, November, 87 : 929, 424–8 and 449.

World Accounting Report (1986) A fair view of what is 'correct', May, 20.

9

Foreign currency capital clauses

CLIVE M. SCHMITTHOFF

This article deals with the following question: can the capital of a company registered under the Companies Act 1985 or any of its predecessors be expressed in a currency other than pounds sterling? The answer depends obviously on the interpretation of the 1985 Act, and in particular of s. 2(5)(a) which reads:

> The memorandum must also (unless it is an unlimited company) state the amount of the share capital with which the company proposes to be registered and the division of the share capital into shares of a fixed amount.

The problem arises in two forms, namely, can the capital clause be expressed in several currencies, that is pounds sterling and a foreign currency (multi-capital clause), or can the capital clause be solely expressed in a foreign currency (foreign currency clause)?

The present examination will consider:

1. Foreign currency clauses in public companies;
2. Foreign currency clauses in private companies;
3. The accounting treatment of foreign currency clauses; and
4. The economic effect of the admission of foreign currency capital clauses by United Kingdom law.

FOREIGN CURRENCY CLAUSES IN PUBLIC COMPANIES

(a) The Scandinavian Bank Group case

Some of the problems under examination were considered by Harman J in *Re Scandinavian Bank Group* [1987] 2 WLR 752. The Scandinavian Bank Group, a public company incorporated in England, is one of the most respected banking institutions in the country and was granted the status of a recognized bank under the Banking Act 1979 (now superseded by the Banking Act 1987). When the matter came before the court the total assets of the bank were nearly £3.3 billion. Technically the matter came before the court on a petition for confirmation of a reduction of capital under s. 136 of the 1985 Act. In substance, however, the court was asked to decide whether it was lawful for the company to divide its capital into four classes of £30m, $30m, SFr 30m and DM30m respectively. There were to be 300m shares respectively of 10p each, 10 US cents each, 10 Swiss centimes each, and 10 pfennigs each. The court was thus asked to approve a reorganization providing for a multi-currency capital clause.

As far as the capital expressed in pounds sterling was concerned, the issued share capital was £64370. This figure is of significance because as regards a public company, s. 45(2)(a) of the 1985 Act provides that the issued capital must be not less than 'the authorized minimum', which is fixed by s. 118(1) at present at £50000. The Scandinavian Bank thus clearly had the authorized minimum prescribed for a public company expressed in pounds sterling, and no difficulty arose on this point.

However, the learned judge, when considering the admissibility of the proposed multi-currency clause, had two hurdles to overcome, both provided by the wording of s. 2(5)(a). The first was that this provision, quoted earlier, used the expression 'amount' in the singular, whereas the various amounts in the proposed multi-currency clause were in the plural, and the second whether the words 'fixed' amount in the section referred only to an amount fixed in pounds sterling.

(b) 'Amount'

Harman J held that the word 'amount' in s. 2(5)(a) meant a monetary amount but it did not mean an amount capable of payment in legal tender. He referred to the fact that a share may be expressed as having a nominal amount of ½p although ½p was abolished as legal tender and in this connection Harman J referred to a decision of Hoffman J in *Re Rotaprint,* which was decided on 21 July 1986 (unreported) after the abolition of the ½p as legal tender. As regards the use of the word 'amount' in the section in the singular, the learned judge referred to the Interpretation Act 1978, according to which the use of the singular includes the plural unless a contrary intention appears from the Act in question. Harman J found that there was no contrary intention to be discovered in the Companies Act. That the words 'amount' or 'amounts' referred to monetary amounts excludes, for example, the fixing of the amount of the capital or a share in troy ounces of gold or in stones of potatoes. It excludes also mere accounting units such as the SDR of the International Monetary Fund or the ECU of the EC.

(c) 'Fixed' amount

Harman J then considered what was meant by the phrase 'fixed' amount of shares. At first glance, it is quite clear that the legislator intends to prohibit no par value shares, in other words shares expressed as a fraction of the capital. But the learned judge also considered the matter from the point of view of the creditor. It was argued against the admission of the multi-currency capital clause that, if the capital was expressed in several currencies, a creditor of the company could never be certain what the capital of the company was and the capital clause would thus defeat its purpose.

The answer to this argument is of utmost importance in company law. Harman J stressed that this argument confused two aspects which should be kept separate, namely the nominal amount of a share and the value of the share. The value depends on the financial situation of the company, its assets and liabilities. It may well be that a share of a nominal amount of 25p is valued by The Stock Exchange at £5 if the company is a listed company. It is the value of the share which matters to the creditor, not its nominal amount. The learned judge said (on p. 763):

> ... I reject the contention that a share has a value, in the sense of a monetary amount to which a shareholder is entitled, or upon which a creditor can truly look as a fixed sum in English pounds. There can be no doubt that the directors of a company can receive subscriptions for shares in a foreign currency – see s. 738(4) of the Act of 1985 which provides that cash includes foreign currency and s. 738(2) of the same Act which provides that receipt in good faith of a cheque is payment-up of the nominal amount (described as 'nominal value') of any share.

(d) The wider view

Harman J supported the conclusion at which he had arrived by pointing out that the House of Lords in *Miliangos* v. *George Frank (Textiles) Ltd* [1976] AC 443 abandoned the long-established rule that an English court could only give a judgment in pounds sterling but held that, if the money of the contract was expressed in a foreign currency, judgment could be given in that currency. The words of the learned judge on this point are worth quoting (on p. 759):

> For myself I do not doubt that there was before and throughout the first half, or perhaps the first two-thirds, of the present century a usually unstated assumption that English companies must have their capital and draw their accounts in English currency. The pound had for so many years been properly called 'a pound sterling'; that is a unit with a value in precious metal. Such a unit may fluctuate in internal purchasing power, but can be taken as having a stated value. But the United Kingdom went off the gold standard many years ago, and has ceased to have any fixed rate of exchange for the pound in any foreign currency since the collapse of the Bretton Woods Agreement in 1971. In these changed circumstances, the law has had to adjust its perceptions so as not to cause injustice to individuals.

(e) Subscription and issue of shares

The creation of a multi-currency capital clause raises a further problem, with which, however, Harman J was not concerned in the *Scandinavian Bank Group* case. The problem is whether such a clause can be inserted into the memorandum on the formation of the company, or only on an increase in capital after the company is formed. The question did not arise in the *Scandinavian Bank Group* case because in this case the multi-currency capital clause was created by increase of the capital on its reorganization.

As regards the subscription on formation of the company the difficulty is created by the Companies (Tables A to F) Regulations 1985 (SI 1985, No. 805). The Tables relating to the memoranda given in Tables B to D and F refer to capital and share amounts in pounds sterling, and not in any foreign currency. Harman J in the *Scandinavian Bank Group* case observed (on p. 764) that it was the practice of the Registrar of Companies, based on advice, to accept increases of capital under s. 121 of the 1985 Act though in a different currency from that of the original share capital. It would, therefore, appear that the Registrar is not willing to register a company having the capital clause expressed in a multi-currency or foreign currency form on formation, his reason probably being the models in the Tables Regulations.

In my view, this differentiation in the treatment of a multi-currency capital clause on subscription and increase is not justified. Section 2(5) (b) and (c), which deal with this topic, do not impose an obligation to provide the ordinary capital in pounds sterling or for the subscription of the shares in that currency, and the Tables have no statutory force; they are only models which should be followed. The only reason why a company formed as a public company must have a pound sterling capital is that it cannot do business and will not be granted a trading certificate unless it has issued shares of the nominal value of the authorized minimum, which at present is £50000; in other words, such a company has to comply with ss. 117 and 118 before commencing business.

On the other hand, if a company is formed as a private company and then converted into a public company, it may, in my view, be formed with a foreign currency clause, but on conversion it must increase its capital by the authorized minimum in pounds sterling, in compliance with s. 45(2)(a) and this would turn it into a multi-currency capital company.

(f) Foreign currency capital clauses in public companies

It follows from the provisions of ss. 117 and 118, discussed before, that it is not possible in the law of the United Kingdom to constitute a public limited company which has exclusively foreign capital. Such a company would contravene the provisions relating to the author-ized minimum. Consequently, in public companies only the multi-currency capital clause is admitted.

It may be added that the fixed amount of a share requirement is not satisfied if the share is expressed in two alternative currencies, e.g. £1 or $1 (Harman J, *loc. cit.*, 763).

FOREIGN CURRENCY CLAUSES IN PRIVATE COMPANIES

(a) The principle

Re Scandinavian Bank Group is no direct authority on the question of whether multi-currency or foreign currency clauses are lawful in private companies. The Act does not prescribe a minimum capital or authorized minimum for private companies; the requirements of ss. 117 and 118 do not apply to them.

The only section which is relevant here is s. 2 (5) (a). As has been seen from the judgment of Harman J in the *Scandinavian Bank Group* case, this section does not provide an obstacle to the admis-sion of multi-currency capital clauses, and what the learned judge said there, with respect to public companies, applies with equal force to private companies. In my view, the Registrar should likewise admit the formation of private companies having a foreign capital but this point, as already observed, is not free from controversy.

(b) The practice

It may perhaps come as a surprise to the reader that in practice

British companies having a foreign capital are not uncommon. Harman J mentioned in the *Scandinavian Bank Group* case that according to the evidence of the Registrar of Companies at least 125 companies have a foreign currency capital and probably two have a multi-currency capital. Indeed, the learned judge referred to the unreported case of *Re Chase Manhattan Ltd.* decided 21 January 1986, an English private company in which he confirmed the reduction of the capital in pounds sterling to nothing and approved an increase in United States dollars. Here is a modern development of company law which is widely unnoticed but, as we shall see, is of great potential future importance.

THE ACCOUNTING TREATMENT OF FOREIGN CURRENCY CLAUSES

Harman J, in the judgment frequently referred to before, fully dealt with the accounting aspects of foreign currency and multi-currency capital clauses. There is no doubt that if a company uses such clauses difficult accounting problems arise.

The main difficulty is to translate the balance sheet of a company having a multi-currency capital into one currency because obviously the balance sheet can be expressed only in one currency, which, however, need not be pounds sterling. The date of the translation should be the date of the balance sheet. The notes to the balance sheet should indicate the particulars and the date of the translation.

In the view of the learned judge, such a translation in the balance sheet, which is required to give a true and fair view, is possible. Harman J referred to the fact that such a translation has to be done on the right-hand side of the balance sheet if the company has foreign currency assets, and he saw no reason why it should not also be done on the left-hand side where the capital of the company is shown. He said (on p. 762):

> No one doubts that accounts must be drawn in one currency. It is probable that if a company has a multi-currency share capital the auditors will translate the left-hand side of the balance sheet into the one currency used for the accounts at rates of exchange ruling at the balance sheet date. Such an observation is equally true of the right-hand side of a balance

sheet. If a company holds assets in Japan, in India, in France and in the United States, but draws its accounts in English pounds, all of those assets will have to be translated into English pounds at the relevant rate of exchange at the balance sheet date. If such a process is proper for the right-hand side of a balance sheet, or for a statement of assets in a narrative form of accounts, I cannot see why it is inappropriate on the left-hand side, or for debits in a narrative form of accounts.

Harman J referred also to three items of evidence in support of his view that a multi-currency capital clause was lawful. First, he mentioned that the well-known firm of chartered accountants who were the auditors of the company were confident that they could assess the accounts with a multi-currency share capital on the true and fair view basis. Secondly, no public authority, notably the Bank of England and the Treasury, was concerned that the decision on the lawfulness of multi-currency capital, which the learned judge reached, would cause them problems. Thirdly, the Official Receiver saw no difficulty in administering liquidations, although he expected, following *Re Lines Bros. Ltd* [1983] Ch 1, to draw up the liquidation account of an insolvent company in sterling, converted at the date of the winding up. Harman J added the gloss that, although the liquidation account must be expressed in a single currency, that currency need not always be pounds sterling.

THE ECONOMIC EFFECT OF THE ADMISSION OF FOREIGN CURRENCY CAPITAL CLAUSES BY UNITED KINGDOM LAW

The economic effect of the admission of multi-currency and foreign currency capital clauses for companies incorporated in the United Kingdom is likely to be enormous. The United Kingdom has always been a popular venue for the incorporation of companies carrying on business internationally. The United Kingdom company law is liberal in spirit, as the decision of Harman J in the *Scandinavian Bank Group* case demonstrates, but it is strict in its requirements of accountability and provides effective remedies of investigation by the public authorities and against dishonest or merely unfit directors or managers. It is widely accepted as striking a fair balance between liberality and strictness.

The popularity of English incorporation for a company intending to carry on business abroad is evidenced by the fact that a famous Parisian restaurant of world reputation, Maxim's, was incorporated as an English company (*Maxim's Ltd* v. *Dye* [1977] 1 WLR 1155, 1157). The capital of Maxim's Ltd was, of course, expressed in pounds sterling, in harmony with the prevailing practice in 1907, when the company was formed. It is not difficult to imagine that, if Maxim's had been constituted today, some 80 years later, it would have been incorporated as an English company having a capital expressed in French francs.

The admission of multi-currency and foreign exchange capital clauses for companies incorporated in the United Kingdom is of particular importance to the company law scene in the EC. Even after the establishment of the single market at the end of 1992 the company laws of the Member States of the EC will not be unified. The aim of the EC is to harmonize and approximate the national company laws of the Member States, but not to unify them. The harmonization of national company laws is done mainly by Directives issued by the Council of Ministers under Article 54(3)(g) of the EC Treaty. It is not necessary to discuss here the numerous Directives already issued by the Council of Ministers; many of them have already been incorporated into the national company laws of the Member States and others will follow suit. But even when the programme of company law harmonization of the EC is further advanced and completed, considerable differences in the company law climate of the various Member States will remain. In some Member States the practical application of the harmonization measures and the general company law will be less strict than in others. By way of illustration, reference may be made to the present treatment of insider dealing in the Member States. In the United Kingdom insider dealing is not only morally reprehensible but is a criminal offence under the Company Securities (Insider Dealing) Act 1985 and, as such, punished with severity. In Italy, on the other hand, the position appears to be different; although at present there is before the Italian Parliament a draft proposal making share trading based on privileged information a criminal offence, the following observations by Alan Friedman in *The Financial Times* of 15 July 1988 are noteworthy:

> Italy remains a country which has no formal company takeover panel and no anti-trust legislation, and the Milan equity market is riddled with the kind of insider trading that would be prosecuted if it took place in London or New York.

This difference in the company law climate of the constituent members of a combination or federation of states is nothing extraordinary. In the United States of America, there is a division of company law. The law relating to the organization of companies is state law and differs considerably in the various states of the federation, but the law relating to securities and investments is federal law and uniform. As far as the organization of companies in the USA is concerned, the law of the state of Delaware is the most lenient law. This has led to the result that many of the leading companies in the USA are incorporated in Delaware, although their seat of business is in another state. Notable here are the Ford Motor Corporation and General Motors, which are corporations incorporated in Delaware but having their seat of business in Detroit in the state of Michigan.

The admission of multi-currency and foreign exchange capital clauses for companies incorporated in the United Kingdom may become an attraction for companies or proposed companies in other parts of the EC to seek incorporation in the United Kingdom. Although, speaking generally, UK company law is in some respects stricter than the company laws of other Member States, incorporation in the United Kingdom carries considerable advantages in the eyes of investors. Apart from the prestige which UK incorporation confers, the strictness of UK company regulations, and particularly the investigatory powers of the authorities, are regarded widely as a safeguard for investments. But more important, incorporation in the United Kingdom paves the way to the admission to one of the markets of the International Stock Exchange in London, which is still one of the financial centres of the world. The markets in question are that for listed securities, the unlisted securities market (USM) and the third market. The admission of multi-currency and foreign exchange capital clauses by the courts, as exemplified by the judgment of Harman J in the *Scandinavian Bank Group* case, is thus a forward-looking decision of great importance; it opens great potentialities for the future.

10

The valuation problem in contemporary financial reporting in the United Kingdom

GEOFFREY WHITTINGTON

INTRODUCTION

It has been fashionable among academic accountants to ridicule the historical cost basis of accounting and those who led the accounting profession to adopt it. But an examination of leading accounting texts of the early years of this century, when accounting conventions were becoming crystallized, shows this to be a cautionary tale of originators who knew what they were doing and of those who came after following blindly the rules laid down without looking behind them. The leaders of professional thought seem to have recognized the relevance of current replacement cost, but to have seen also substantial practical difficulties in measuring it. And so they decided that in the circumstances of that time, historical cost would give, in most instances, a good approximation to current cost without the trouble of measuring the latter. Since that time circumstances have changed, but historical cost accounting remains – admittedly with some modifications.

(Bird, 1979, p. 41)

This characteristically clear and perceptive comment by Peter Bird provides the context of this paper. Accounting practice has evolved around the principle of valuing assets at their historical cost, i.e. at what was paid for them. This method has the apparent virtue of objectivity: historical cost arises from a transaction and all that the accountant or auditor needs to ascertain it is to check the details of the transaction. Current valuation bases, such as current replacement cost, suffer, on the other hand, from the apparent problem of subjectivity: to ascertain current values, the accountant or auditor is required to conduct a hypothetical exercise to establish what *would* have been paid for the asset had it been acquired at the date of valuation. Moreover, at times when prices are stable, the difference between historical cost and current cost is likely to be small and therefore inadequate to provide an incentive for the preparer of accounts to incur the additional expense and risk of estimating current costs. Thus traditional historical cost accounting has a sound rationale in conditions of price stability and when current costs are difficult (i.e. expensive and uncertain) to obtain relative to historical costs. It is also the case that the benefit obtained from current cost information may depend upon the need and sophistication of the user of accounts. For some purposes, it may be that historical cost is adequate, providing a relatively objective record of past transactions, and for others it may be that, although accurate current cost measures would be ideal, the unsophisticated user is unable to make good use of them or may even be misled by relying too heavily on current cost measures which, in practice, are unlikely to be precise. However, it does seem likely that, in the hands of a sophisticated user, current cost information would be more relevant than historical cost information in assessing the current economic state of a business.

The rapid changes in prices in recent years, particularly in the mid 1970s, have weakened the case for historical cost accounting by increasing the gap between historical cost and current cost. In these conditions, it cannot reasonably be argued that historical cost is a good proxy for current cost, especially in the case of long-lived assets, for which the gap between historical cost and current cost grows greater as the asset's life grows longer. In such circumstances, the accountant becomes vulnerable to the criticism that his information is precisely correct but totally irrelevant. Furthermore, the pressure of rising prices can lead to historical cost profits being inflated, relative to current cost profits, so that firms find themselves under pressure from government to limit prices and pay heavy taxes and from trade unions to grant high wage increases. These factors combined in the mid 1970s to encourage firms to take a more favourable view of current cost accounting than had been the case previously.

The history of price change accounting in the United Kingdom is well known (see Tweedie and Whittington (1984)) and requires only the briefest description here. As the rate of inflation rose in the late 1960s and early 1970s, the accounting profession began to favour the implementation of constant purchasing power accounting (CPP) in supplementary financial statements, for dealing with the problem of general inflation. This was proposed by the Accounting Standards Steering Committee (ASSC) in an exposure draft (ED 8, 1973) and then adopted in a provisional standard (PSSAP 7, 1974). CPP involves general index adjustment of historical costs and therefore fails to address the problem of different relative changes in the prices of specific assets. It was probably this deficiency which led the government to intervene by appointing the Sandilands Committee, which, in its Report (1975), recommended current cost accounting, revaluing all assets on a specific 'value to the business' basis, and making no use of general indices. This system was to replace historical cost in the main accounts. The Accounting Standards Committee was given the responsibility of implementing a system of price change accounting which reflected the Sandilands proposals. After much painful debate, a current cost accounting standard, SSAP 16, was finally implemented in 1980. Its four major differences from Sandilands were, first, that it required only supplementary disclosure; secondly, that it applied only to large companies; thirdly that it included a gearing adjustment intended to capture the gain on borrowing in a period of rising prices; and fourthly that it included a monetary working capital adjustment intended to reflect the loss on holding monetary assets (or alternatively the greater nominal amount of the monetary working capital requirement) when prices rise. These differences reflect the most contentious issues in the debate.

SSAP 16 was, at first, implemented by most large companies and nearly all of those with a Stock Exchange listing. However, the environment changed: prices became more stable (although general inflation was and still is high by historical standards), the corporation tax system was changed in ways which made it clear that the implementation of price change accounting was unlikely to have any implication for tax relief, and the advent of a government committed to market solutions of economic problems meant that prices and dividend controls were abandoned. There was also some disenchantment with CCA due to difficulties of implementation and apparent lack of interest by users. The net effect of all this was a dramatic falling away of support for CCA, culminating in the effective abandonment of SSAP 16 in 1985, with the substitution of a purely advisory handbook on *Accounting for the Effects of Changing Prices* (ASC, 1986). Thus, the popularity of price change accounting has reached a low ebb in the private sector and in professional circles, although the publication of the Byatt Report (HM Treasury Advisory Group, 1986) shows that the issue of current cost accounting is still an important one in the public sector. Moreover, many of the arguments of the Byatt Report are equally relevant to the private sector, and the spectacle of nationalized industries switching from CCA to historical cost accounting when they are privatized has raised awkward questions about whether the switch really led to the accounts giving a better picture of the economic substance of the entity concerned.

The object of this paper is not to attempt a theoretical justification of the introduction of current costs into accounts in preference to historical costs: the present author has attempted this elsewhere (Whittington, 1983). Rather, the object is to develop the theme that the problem of valuation, and particularly the choice between current and historical costs as the basis of valuation, is still present and underlies many current accounting standards. The problem has not disappeared, it has merely been driven underground. One of the reasons why preparers of accounts seem happy with this situation is that they are, in some important instances, given a choice of current or historical valuation, and at a time when cosmetic reporting is rampant (for example, see Griffiths (1986)) this may be more attractive than a prescriptive regime which allows no choice.

The paper proceeds as follows: the following section deals with the legal framework, defined by the Companies Act 1985. The next section provides the main evidence by means of a systematic exploration of the valuation methods allowed by current accounting standards. The final section draws together the main themes and indicates some conclusions.

THE LEGAL FRAMEWORK

Company accounts in the United Kingdom are regulated by the Companies Act 1985, which consolidates earlier Acts. The Act specifies four fundamental *accounting principles*, which are consistent with those specified earlier by the ASSC in SSAP 2 (1971). These are the going concern assumption, consistency in application of accounting policies, prudence, and the accruals principle. Prudence includes the assumption that the profit and loss account should include revenue or profit only when realized in the form of cash or other assets which have a reasonably certain cash value. However, this does not prevent current values from being reported in the balance sheet. In so far as revaluations create gains, these can be credited direct to a capital reserve rather than being passed through the profit and loss account. This has the effect of changing the capital maintenance concept upon which the profit calculation is based.

The Act also contains two sets of *accounting rules*, the historical cost accounting rules and the alternative accounting rules. The latter rules apply when a historical cost basis is not used for valuation purposes and, in practice, many companies use a mixture of historical cost and current valuation. This is, of course, a major source of the valuation problem in current accounting practice. However, it is worth noting that even under the strict historical cost rules, current valuations are not necessarily absent, for two reasons. First, the prudence principle requires valuation at historical cost or market value, whichever is the lower, so that historical cost will typically be replaced by current value when that is the lower (with some qualifications: for example, in the case of fixed assets the diminution of value would have to be permanent for a write-down to recoverable amount to be obligatory). Secondly, there are three specific instances in which current values are required to be reported when they are materially different from historical cost: the Directors' Report must report substantial differences between the book value and the market value of land (including buildings thereon); the market value of listed securities must be stated by way of a note to the balance sheet, when it differs from the amount appearing on the face of the balance sheet; and the replacement cost of stocks should be stated in a note to the balance sheet when it is materially different from book value. These adjustments suggest that, in cases in which market values can be established with reasonable certainty, the legislators and their advisers prefer current values to historical costs, or at least attach equal importance to them. This suggests that it is the practical problem of establishing current values objectively, rather than doubts about their relevance, which stands in the way of their adoption. This lends credence to the argument advanced by Peter Bird in the passage which prefaces this paper.

The 1985 Companies Act contains another accounting provision which is important in providing grounds for the discretionary use of current values and which also is of fundamental importance to the work of the Accounting Standards Committee (ASC). This is the doctrine of *the true and fair view*. All company accounts are required to give a true and fair view, and this requirement can lead to the provision of information additional to that prescribed in the Act and may even override the other disclosure requirements of the Act (s. 228(5)). This provision is extremely important for the work of the ASC. Accounting standards can be regarded as defining accounting policies which meet the requirements of the 'true and fair view', and this has provided ASC's justification for recommending a number of departures from the strict letter of the Companies Act requirements (such as the relaxation of the depreciation requirement in the case of investment properties in SSAP 19). At a late stage in the current cost accounting debate (1984), the ASC even contemplated requiring disclosure of current cost information as part of the notes to the main accounts, on the ground that this was necessary for the presentation of a true and fair view, and obtained counsel's opinion that such a requirement by the ASC would carry weight in any litigation concerning the content of accounts.

In summary, the accounting framework prescribed by the 1985 Companies Act contains a great deal of flexibility with respect to the valuation basis of accounts, despite the Act's apparently detailed accounting requirements. Thus, responsibility for improving the comparability of the accounts of different companies by standardizing practice and limiting the choice of accounting methods has fallen to the ASC, and it is to the ASC's standard-setting programme which we now turn.

ACCOUNTING STANDARDS

(a) Fixed assets

The most obvious case in which the valuation problem enters company accounts is in the valuation of fixed assets. Because such assets are durable, their life typically spans several accounting periods and the gap between historical cost and current cost may be high. As we have already seen, the Companies Act is permissive on the question of valuation base, so that the law allows a wide variety of practice, piecemeal revaluation of a sub-set of the fixed assets on an irregular basis being quite common. A good survey of current practice is provided by Macdonald (1987). Clearly, this form of modified historical cost accounting, with its wide range of discretion in valuation matters makes inter-company comparisons difficult and it is perhaps surprising that the ASC has not, as yet, provided guidance on the circumstances in which revaluation is considered appropriate, although the topic is on the ASC's agenda for future work.

The ASC has, however, dealt with certain specific aspects of fixed asset valuation. Most notably, it has addressed the problem of depreciation in SSAP 12. The Companies Act 1985 requires all fixed assets of limited life to be depreciated over their lifetimes, and SSAP 12 clarifies the principles upon which this should be done. The fact that it has been revised twice (in 1981 and 1987) shows that this is a controversial issue, but the main controversy has been not about the amount of depreciation deducted from the asset's cost or value in the balance sheet, but about the amount of depreciation charged to the profit and loss account. The bone of contention here is the concept of *capital maintenance* which parallels that of valuation in the process of assessing profit, i.e. the question is the extent of the charge to be made against profit for the use of fixed assets during a period of time. Clearly, the higher the value at which the asset is stated, the greater will be the future depreciation. However, the effect of this on profit is ambiguous, for two reasons.

First, there is the issue of whether a revaluation of an asset should be regarded as giving rise to a gain which should appear in the profit and loss account, and, if so, the precise extent to which this should occur. Company law suggests that unrealized gains on assets should be credited to an undistributable revaluation reserve, but there are a number of 'grey' areas here, notably the question of whether previously charged depreciation can be written back to profit and loss to the extent that it has written the book value of the asset to below current value. Another contentious issue is whether losses on holding certain assets can be offset agains gains on holding other assets of a similar type, rather than being charged against profit.

Secondly, there is the issue of whether subsequent depreciation on the revalued asset should all be charged to the profit and loss account, or whether depreciation on the element of revaluation should be debited direct to revaluation reserve, as in the celebrated Woolworth split depreciation method. The latter approach is now ruled out by the recent (1987) revision of SSAP 12. The issue of capital maintenance is, of course, an extremely important one in current accounting standards and underlies the whole issue of reserve accounting, which has, in turn, been one of the central strands in the problem of creative accounting in recent years (see Griffiths (1986)). To explain the extent of the problem at all adequately would require a separate paper, and all that can be done here is to emphasize its complementarity with the valuation problem. Despite its failure, hitherto, to provide a general guidance on fixed assets revaluation, the ASC has given guidance on the valuation of fixed assets in two specific areas: 'fair value' in acquisition accounting (SSAP 14) and the valuation of investment properties (SSAP 19).

(b) Fair value in acquisition accounting

'Fair value' (SSAP 14) is a concept which arises in consolidated accounts of groups of companies. When one company acquires a controlling interest in another, there are three possible accounting treatments. First, the new company may not be consolidated in the accounts of the holding company if it fulfils certain legal criteria. This is relatively rare and is currently a contentious issue, forming part of the 'off balance sheet financing' controversy (see Griffiths (1986), Chapter 14, and Brindle (1987), which ED 42 is intended to resolve, by insisting that the economic substance of the relationship should be reported in order that the accounts give a true and fair view. Secondly, the two companies may be treated on a pooling of interests basis, when the relationship can be treated as a merger rather than an acquisition. This implies that the assets of the acquired company will be taken into the group accounts at their book value, rather than being revalued. This approach, 'merger accounting', has also been a contentious subject during the recent controversy on creative accounting (see Griffiths (1986), Chapter 8, and Wild (1987)). The third approach, which is the most common, is 'acquisition accounting', and it is this which gives rise to the problem of fair value.

In acquisition accounting, the newly acquired subsidiary's assets are re-stated at 'fair value' for group accounting purposes. The value of net assets acquired (assets less liabilities) assessed on this basis is then compared with the market value of the consideration paid (cash and/or shares) and any surplus of consideration over net assets acquired is treated as 'goodwill', an intangible asset whose treatment is prescribed by SSAP 23 (conversely 'negative goodwill', a surplus of net assets acquired over consideration paid, is treated as an undistributable reserve). Goodwill is required to be written off immediately against reserves, or over its useful economic life by an amortization charge which appears as an expense in the profit and loss account. Some ingenious methods have been evolved by which goodwill can be offset against various reserves, rather than becoming a charge against future profits. On the other hand, depreciating assets which have been revalued at fair value must be depreciated on their full amount over their lifetimes, and this will be a charge against future profits (SSAP 12, revised). Thus, there is an incentive for holding companies to assess the fair value of newly acquired subsidiaries' assets as low as possible and to make the maximum possible provision for restructuring costs and similar potential liabilities, thus leaving the highest possible proportion of the purchase consideration to be recorded as goodwill, which will not necessarily impose a burden on future profits. For this reason, and, more generally, in order to clarify and give guidance to enable more consistent application of the fair value concept, the ASC currently has fair value on its agenda of new accounting standards. For the purposes of the present essay, it is sufficient to note that fair value introduces an element of current valuation into group accounts. This can, of course, be interpreted as 'historical cost at the time of acquisition of the subsidiary', but it is certainly a current valuation relative to the merger accounting approach, which records the assets at historical cost at the time of acquisition of the asset by the subsidiary.

(c) The valuation of investment properties

SSAP 19 (1981) defines a category of investment properties, land and buildings which are held for investment purposes, rather than for the owning company's own occupation. Such properties can be held by any type of company, not merely property investment companies, although the latter are obviously the main target of SSAP 19. It requires that investment properties should be valued at current open market value in the balance sheet, that no depreciation should be provided on them (except in the case of fixed-term leasehold property), and that changes in value should be taken direct to a revaluation reserve rather than passing through the profit and loss account. With regard to depreciation, this represents a departure from the Companies Act requirement to provide for depreciation on any fixed asset which has a limited useful economic life, and this is justified by an appeal by the ASC to the overriding requirement to provide a true and fair view.

Clearly, in this particular instance, the ASC was on fairly safe ground in appealing to the true and fair override, because the group of preparers of accounts which was most affected, the property investment companies, was likely to support SSAP 19. Without the exemption from depreciation charges, property companies which had invested for growth of capital value rather than high rentals might have found their rental income wiped out by depreciation charges, so that they had no distributable profit, despite a good capital appreciation performance.

Two aspects of SSAP 19 are worthy of particular note in relation to the central theme of this essay. First, SSAP 19 provides a case in which the need to express economic reality has, through appeal to the true and fair view, been allowed to lead to a requirement for current value to appear in the balance sheet and for the legal requirement for a depreciation charge in the profit and loss account to be overridden. The latter could be interpreted as a crude attempt to introduce an element of unrealized capital gain into the profit and loss account since the reason for eliminating depreciation is, presumably, that it is typically offset by capital appreciation. (The New Zealand standard equivalent to SSAP 19. addresses this problem more directly by allowing the unrealized gain in value to be shown as a separate item in the income statement.) Secondly, SSAP 19 applies only to investment properties, presumably because the main pressure for its provisions came from property investment companies, but it is difficult conceptually to justify the distinction between properties held for investment and properties held for the company's own use. Properties held for investment do typically yield a rent, whereas properties held for own use do not, but the latter do lead to the avoidance of the need to pay a rent, which represents just as real an economic return. Indeed, divisionalized firms may well charge an internal rent to divisions for the use of property, but this will not allow them to regard the property as an investment property under SSAP 19. Equally, property will not change its economic life or its pattern of capital value through time merely because it is owner-occupied rather than rented out, and it is therefore difficult to justify the exemption of investment properties alone from the depreciation charge.

(d) The valuation of leases

An interesting recent development in the valuation of fixed assets relates to leases. Leasing has become a popular method of financing in recent years, initially because of tax incentives, and latterly as a method of financing which allows both the asset and the source of finance to be left off the lessee's balance sheet, thus improving the apparent liquidity and gearing of the company. Leasing was thus an early manifestation of the off balance sheet financing phenomenon, and it was the first to be dealt with (SSAP 21, 1984).

The way in which SSAP 21 dealt with leases was to distinguish between operating and financing leases. Operating leases are more in the nature of rental contracts and it is sufficient that the accounts should show the rental charge in the profit and loss account, together with a note to the balance sheet to indicate any future obligations or contingencies arising from the contract. Financing leases, on the other hand, involve the lessee in effectively taking on most of the economic benefits and obligations of ownership, and it is these which previously could have been regarded as giving rise to off balance sheet financing. Under SSAP 21, however, finance leases must be dealt with by recording the leased asset, at fair value at the date of purchase, together with subsequent depreciation, in the accounts of the lessee. Correspondingly, the liability for future lease payments is shown, at its discounted present value, in the lessee's balance sheet, and subsequent payments under the lease are to be apportioned between capital repayment and interest on an actuarial basis (or one of the approximations to this prescribed by the standard).

The SSAP 21 treatment of finance leases is, of course, entirely consistent with historical cost accounting. The asset is recorded at 'fair value', i.e. an open market value, at the time of its effective acquisition (the date of commencement of the lease). However, two features of the SSAP 21 provisions are worthy of note from the point of view of our central theme, the valuation problem.

First, by introducing fair value at the time of acquisition, for asset valuation, and by using discounting methods for measuring the liability for future payments under the lease, SSAP 21 uses techniques which are fundamental to a systematic application of current value or current cost accounting. Admittedly, 'fair value' is assessed only at the time of acquisition, rather than being reassessed annually, thus maintaining the historical cost principle, and the actuarial discounting method of assessing liabilities is applied in conditions of

162

unusual certainty, the future obligations being clearly defined by the lease contract. Nevertheless, the use of these methods does imply that the techniques themselves are not impractical or unacceptable. Any argument that current values cannot be implemented in accounting practice must therefore rest on the unreliability of the basic data, for example it may be that more information is available at the time of acquisition, facilitating the estimation of fair value at this particular time, and it is also undoubtedly the case that future cash flows attaching to assets or liabilities are rarely defined with the degree of certainty created by a lease contract.

A second important aspect of SSAP 21 is the reasoning behind the proposals. Essentially, SSAP 21 asserts the need to present a true and fair view of the economic substance of the business, rather than merely being concerned with the strict legal form of ownership of the assets. Once we are concerned to define assets as rights to economic benefits rather than historical legal claims, it is not at all clear that the economic substance of the business is best described by valuing those benefits only at the time of acquisition, rather than showing current values which reflect economic events subsequent to acquisition. It was, of course, this type of argument which the ASC was, at one time, prepared to invoke in support of its proposed current cost standard (ED 35, 1984).

(e) Stocks and work in progress

Hitherto, we have concentrated on the valuation of fixed assets. The component of current assets which gives rise to the greatest valuation problem is stocks and work in progress, which is dealt with by SSAP 9 (revised September 1988).

We have already seen that, under the 1985 Companies Act, the valuation principle under the conventional accounting rules is cost or market value (interpreted, in the case of stocks, as net realizable value), whichever is the lower, and that an additional note is required where replacement cost differs materially from this. An important element in stock valuation is the flow-through assumption used to identify the items in closing stock: the Companies Act permits LIFO (last in, first out) and other methods (such as base stock).

The stock flow-through assumption is an interesting illustration of the relationship between valuation and capital maintenance. FIFO is often preferred as giving the more realistic valuation of closing stock for balance sheet purposes, the closing stock being valued at the cost of the most recently acquired purchases, which is likely to be closest to current value. On the other hand, LIFO is sometimes preferred as giving a more realistic charge for cost of sales in the profit and loss account: under LIFO the more recent purchases are regarded as sold during the period. The obverse of this is that FIFO tends, by charging old prices, to give an out-of-date charge to profit and loss, whereas LIFO gives an out-of-date valuation of stocks in the balance sheet. Thus, stock appreciation (the rise in value of stocks) is included in closing stock values under FIFO but charged against profit under LIFO.

Clearly, if we believe that current prices are more realistic than historical prices, we would prefer to value closing stock at something like its FIFO valuation (including stock appreciation) and cost of sales under something like LIFO (charging stock appreciation against profit). This ideal solution is achieved in current cost accounting (CCA) by abandoning the concept of maintaining capital in money terms. Thus, in CCA, closing stock is valued at its current cost (closer to FIFO than LIFO) but the cost of goods sold is increased by a cost of sales adjustment, reflecting stock appreciation. In double entry terms, the cost of sales adjustment is debited to cost of sales and credited to a revaluation reserve in the balance sheet. The effect of this is to increase the capital which the business requires to maintain before recognizing a profit. However, CCA is currently in disfavour and it is quite possible that a surge in prices would lead to pressure to adopt LIFO in order to improve the realism of the profit and loss account, at the cost of making the balance sheet less realistic.

An important element in stocks, particularly in manufacturing firms, is work in progress, i.e. partly completed products. The valuation of this item leads inevitably to difficulties in attributing overhead charges, which SSAP 9 tries to clarify, but these would apply under almost any method of valuation (other than immediate sale value, which would not be a realistic option for many part-completed products). Of more interest for the theme of the present essay is the issue of contract work in progress, where an element of profit may be included in the valuation. This is a long-standing tradition in industries such as construction and shipbuilding, in which major projects may span several accounting periods, leading to a very uneven time profile of profit recognition if completion of the contract is taken as the criterion for recognition. SSAP 9 supports the recognition of profits on such contracts before completion, in appropriate circumstances, and this does, of course, represent a step away from historical cost and towards the greater economic reality of current values.

A feature of the revision of SSAP 9 which was proposed in ED 40 (1987) is that a long-term contract which includes an element of profit and which is not covered by progress payments received must now be treated as a debtor 'amount recoverable on contracts' rather than a physical asset (ED 40, Appendix 3). This is partly designed to bring the UK into harmony with international practice and is partly a concession to the Companies Act requirement that current assets should be stated in the balance sheet at purchase price for net realizable value only if lower (preface to ED 40, para. 1.3). It is argued that, if a profit on a long-term contract is certain enough to be treated as realized in the profit and loss account, then the corresponding asset which the company shows in its balance sheet is not a physical asset, work in progress, but a liability by the customer to pay for it.

(f) Pension costs (ED 39 and SSAP 24)

The valuation problem applies to claims *on* a company as much as to assets (which are claims *by* the company). A recent concern of the ASC has been with liabilities for pensions, dealt with the ED 39 and a new Standard: SSAP 24 (May 1988). The central problem in recent years has been the 'pension holiday' which occurs when firms choose not to make contributions for a period because the pension fund appears, on actuarial valuation, to be in surplus, i.e. the value of its resources exceeds its obligations to pensioners in a 'defined benefit' scheme (where benefits are not defined, surpluses cannot occur because the whole fund accrues to the pensioners). Because many companies charge contributions to profit and loss account, the absence of contributions leads to a higher profit figure. The new proposal is that, apart from certain exceptional cases, companies should provide for pension costs on an *accruals* basis rather than a cash basis, i.e. the charge to profit and loss should be based on spreading the ultimate pension cost over the whole employment lives of present employees, so that 'holidays' should not arise because adjustments are spread over longer periods.

From the point of view of our central theme of valuation, the pension cost proposals have the interesting property of looking to the *future* as well as the past. The actuarial calculations which underlie these measurements of cost in the profit and loss account and the associated provisions or liabilities in the balance sheet are, of course, discounted cash flow calculations of a type which accountants have been reluctant to employ in other contexts. However, there is no doubt that actuarial calculations are an essential part of pension fund management, and that, whatever the limitations of our knowledge about the future, such calculations must be and are made in order to give a realistic picture of the present state of a fund: even pension holidays were taken with the support of actuarial evidence.

(g) Deferred tax

The basis of assessment for corporation tax is not reported profits of a company. Differences therefore arise between the corporation tax actually payable on a year's profits and the amount which would have been payable had the year's reported profits been the basis of assessment. A common source of this difference in recent years has been deferral of income recognition for tax purposes due, for example, to capital allowances which, by giving a more rapid depreciation for tax purposes than is given in the accounts, have tended to lead to a deferral of taxation (a 'timing difference') too late in the asset's life, when the asset is written off for tax purposes but not for accounting purposes (when the difference reverses).

There are three basic methods of accounting for deferred taxes. At one extreme, the *flow-through* method ignores deferred tax and merely records the actual tax payable on a particular year's profits. The danger of this method is that it may fail to reveal a tendency to store up heavy tax bills for the future through deferral. At the other extreme, the *full provision* method, currently preferred in the USA, charges the profit and loss account with the full tax which would have been payable in a year had there been no deferral (i.e. had there been no timing difference between the recognition of profit for accounting and for tax purposes). Under this method, the deferred element in the tax charge is credited to a deferred tax provision in the balance sheet, and the transaction is reversed when the timing difference ultimately reverses so that the actual tax charge exceeds that which is made on the basis of accounting profit. The third method is the *partial provision* approach, and this is the method favoured in the UK (SSAP 15, revised 1985). Under this method, provision for deferred tax is made only to the extent that reversal *of the provision can reasonably be foreseen.*

The interesting feature of this from the perspective of the valuation problem is that current UK practice essentially requires a subjective current valuation of the provision, based upon assumptions about future events. An oddity of the current standard is that discounting of future liabilities is not advocated (although it is not ruled out), in contrast with the practice with respect to liabilities for payments under finance leases and for pension obligations.

(h) Complex capital issues

A recent product of the increasing sophistication of capital markets has been an increasing variety and complexity in the terms upon which capital can be arranged. The reporting of these transactions poses a new challenge to accountants and this has not yet been addressed publicly by the ASC, although the ICAEW has issued an advisory Technical Release (TR 677) on the subject.

One of the simpler examples of a complex capital issue is the *stepped interest bond.* This is a loan stock which has variable interest over its lifetime, e.g. it may have a low interest rate in the early years and a rising rate in later years. The way in which TR 677 proposes that this should be dealt with is consistent with the approach to pension costs: rather than the profit and loss account being charged with the cash payment, the total cost of the finance should be spread evenly over its lifetime, using discounting methods. Another such type of issue is the *deep discount bond* which carries a low interest rate but is issued at a discount, so that the gain on ultimate redemption compensates for the low interest rate. In this case too, TR 677 advocates a forward-looking discounted cash flow approach: the discount is to be treated as a 'rolled-up interest charge', and written off over the life of the bond by means of a constant annual charge to the profit and loss account.

Thus, the approach to complex capital issues, as embodied in TR 677, provides yet another area in which, in implementing accrual accounting, accountants are prepared to estimate future cash flows and apply discounted cash flow techniques to estimate the present value of future obligations. It also represents another case in which economic substance is treated as the most important factor in determining how transactions should be reported.

(i) Foreign currency translation

Foreign currency translation may not, superficially, seem to relate to valuation: it may seem to be a purely technical and rather arcane area. However, a little reflection reveals that this is clearly not the case: foreign currency translation determines the valuation, in domestic currency, of all assets, liabilities and transactions in foreign currency. This becomes obvious when we consider the origins of CPP accounting, which was conceived as a method of currency translation into units of constant purchasing power (originally, the gold mark in Germany in the hyperinflation of the early 1920s). CPP typically (in its *current* purchasing power form) uses what is known as the *closing rate method* of currency translation, i.e. all assets and liabilities denominated in foreign currency at the end of an accounting period, and foreign currency transactions during it, are translated into domestic currency at the rate of exchange prevailing at the end of the period (in the case of CPP, 'foreign currency' is equivalent to actual currency, and the CPP unit of constant value is the domestic currency). A variant of this is to translate profit and loss items (i.e. transactions of revenue account during the period) at the *average* rate for the period. It will be recalled from the earlier discussion of CPP that it updates historical cost valuations to allow for changes in the general price level (or, in the foreign currency translation application, changes in the rate of exchange), but it makes no adjustment for the *relative* price changes of specific assets which do not have a fixed monetary value (non-monetary assets). This same deficiency arises in the case of the application of the same technique to foreign currency translation.

Current UK standard practice (SSAP 20, 1983) follows the CPP principle in so far as it relates to the consolidation of foreign subsidiaries into the group accounts of domestic holding companies. The method advocated is the 'closing rate/net investment method', which applies the exchange rate prevailing at the date of the closing balance sheet. It is permitted to use the average rate for the period to translate profit and loss account items, and again this is a variation commonly permitted in CPP accounting.

With regard to foreign currency transactions by domestic companies, SSAP 20 adopts a rather different posture. The method advocated is the 'temporal method' of currency translation, the foreign currency translation method which is logically consistent with the historical cost approach. Transactions are translated from foreign to domestic currency at the rate prevailing *at the time of the transaction*, i.e. at historical cost in terms of domestic currency. In the closing balance sheet, non-monetary assets are valued by reference to the rate of exchange prevailing at the time of acquisition, thus adhering to the strict principle of historical cost in terms of domestic currency. However, a departure from historical cost purity is made in the case of monetary assets and liabilities denominated in foreign currency. These are translated at the rate of exchange prevailing at the closing balance sheet date, and any loss or gain resulting from this restatement process is to appear as part of the ordinary profit calculation in the profit and loss account. This even applies to long-term liabilities, the gain (or loss) on which cannot be regarded as being realized. This is, of course, contrary to the detailed provision of the 1985 Companies Act and the Standard (para. 65) appeals to the need to show a true and fair view as 'a special reason for the departure from the principle' that only realized profits should be passed through the profit and loss account.

Thus, the current standard on foreign currency translation (SSAP 20) contains two broad approaches to the translation problem, and each involves a degree of departure from the strict principle of historical cost, in so far as changes in the price of one currency in terms of another are recognized when they take place between the time of the historical transaction and the closing balance sheet date. Of the two approaches, the one which is most consistent with CCA or other forms of current value accounting is the closing rate method, used in group accounting.

(j) Off balance sheet financing

The problem of off balance sheet financing may, like that of foreign currency translation, seem superficially to have little or nothing to do with valuation. The central problem has been ably described elsewhere (Brindle, 1986 and 1987; Griffiths, 1986; and Tweedie, 1987): various devices have emerged whereby assets and their associated liabilities are not, in legal form, assets and liabilities of the company which benefits from them or bears their economic burden. The ASC has recently published its proposals for dealing with the problem (ED 42, March 1988) and it is the nature of the proposed solution which is relevant to our central theme of valuation.

The central thrust of the ASC's approach to the problem of off balance sheet financing (or, in the ASC's description, 'special purpose transactions') is to emphasize concepts and principles, rather than to try to legislate in detail on individual schemes. This is a sensible approach on practical grounds, since detailed legislation might lead to even more complex avoidance schemes. The central concept of an asset, adopted in ED 42, is as a claim to economic benefits, and, conversely, a liability involves an obligation to part with economic resources. Using these concepts, we can penetrate the complexities of off balance sheet schemes by asking the simple questions 'what are the claims to economic benefit?' (the assets) and 'what are the economic burdens?' (the liabilities). These should be reported in the balance sheet, even if legal ownership of a physical asset does not yet exist and the legal liability has not yet crystallized. Clearly, there is an analogy here with the treatment of finance leases under SSAP 21. This is not surprising, since finance leases are a form of off balance sheet financing which happened to become important rather earlier than other forms and was therefore dealt with earlier by the ASC.

The relevance to the theme of valuation is also similar to that of the finance lease problem. ED 42 provides yet another example of the ASC preferring economic substances over legal form (although it is careful not to spell this out in such stark terms, possibly for fear of offending the lawyers). In identifying economic substance, it is necessary to look to *future* benefits and obligations and this is a step towards accepting the case for some form of current valuation, although ED 42 is careful not to take this final step, preferring to emphasize that its proposals are based on historical cost valuation. However, there may be some inconsistency in using the future to assess whether an economic benefit (or burden) exists, and then using the past to measure the amount of that economic benefit (or burden).

CONCLUSIONS

Our survey of current financial reporting practices in the UK has revealed that the system in place is far removed from pure historical cost accounting, although equally it cannot be claimed, since the demise of SSAP 16, that there is any systematic application of CCA or any other form of current value accounting. Rather, the system is a pragmatic hybrid, with different methods of valuation being preferred for different types of transaction, and with a considerable degree of choice being allowed to the individual preparer of accounts.

With regard to the Companies Act 1985, there are three important types of provision which allow comprehensive or selective deviation from the historical cost principle. First, the alternative accounting rules *permit* current valuation methods throughout the accounts. Secondly, there are certain specific *requirements* that current valuations be reported, e.g. in the case of listed investments. Thirdly, there is an overriding requirement that the accounts give a true and fair view, which allows deviations from specific requirements of the Companies Act and has been invoked on a number of occasions by the ASC.

With regard to current accounting standards, we have considered nine current standards, one exposure draft and one technical release all of which deal with valuation problems and whose recommended solutions contain elements of current valuation. This list is not comprehensive: only the more obvious valuation problems have been examined. Amongst the themes which have emerged from this examination are:

1. A willingness to resort to regular revaluations on a current basis when reliable information is available and there is support from preparers of accounts. This arises particularly in the case of investment properties (SSAP 19), but it also arises more pervasively in the permissive attitude to the revaluation of fixed assets, which the ASC has hitherto not attempted to control or regulate.

2. A willingness to resort to current valuation on specific events, which are not necessarily associated with a market transaction which gives rise to an explicit open market price. This is most obvious in the resort to fair value in acquisition accounting (SSAP 14 and SSAP 23) and in accounting for finance leases (SSAP 21). It is also implicit in the inclusion of unrealized profit in the valuation of work in progress under SSAP 9 and the attainment of a similar result (by early recognition as part of turnover, and the creation of 'amounts recoverable on contracts') in ED 40 and the revised SSAP 9.

3. A willingness to estimate future cash flows for the purposes of valuation of liabilities and provisions. In the case of deferred tax (SSAP 15), this is not combined with a recommendation that the cash flows should be discounted, but such a recommendation is made in the case of pension costs (SSAP 24) (since actuarial methods are used), leases (SSAP 21), and complex capital issues (TR 677). The use of future cash flows in these cases does not necessarily imply a departure from historical cost, for example in the case of a part-expired finance lease it is clearly an attempt to put the calculation of unexpired historical cost on a rational basis. However, it does imply that, at least in some situations, accountants are able to do valuation exercises based on the same theoretical principles as one of the components of the CCA valuation method, the recoverable amount. Objections to the practical difficulties of implementing the CCA valuation principles, particularly the estimation of the recoverable amount, were an important element in the opposition to CCA throughout

the price change accounting debate. Indeed, SSAP 16 shied away from recommending that recoverable amount should be calculated using discounting methods because of the opposition which such a recommendation would have aroused.

4. In the case of foreign currency translation (SSAP 20) a departure from the historical cost principle (the temporal method) is used in group accounts, so that changes in exchange rates subsequent to the acquisition of assets are recognized (the closing rate method). In the case of accounts of individual companies, a method more consistent with historical cost principles is used, but monetary assets and liabilities are still translated at the closing rate, which is not compatible with pure historical cost, even to the extent of recognizing exchange rate gains on long-term liabilities.

5. In standards generally, but particularly in the recent proposals relating to off balance sheet financing (ED 42) and complex capital issues (TR 677) and in the standard on leasing (SSAP 21), there is a concern that accounts should portray the economic substance of the business and its transactions. An attempt has been made (notably in ED 42) to use economic substance arguments to justify the inclusion of an asset or claim in the accounts, but then to record the item at historical cost. If prices have changed materially since the acquisition of the asset or claim, it is difficult to accept that the economic substance of the business is best conveyed by historical costs rather than prices ruling at the date of the balance sheet.

In summary, there are many departures from the historical cost principle, and these are not in a uniform direction. The nature of the variations probably depends on the precise information which is available in each case. For example, it is clear that investment properties are easier to revalue on a regular basis than part-used machinery and the information about future cash flows relating to leases is particularly precise and lends itself to discounted cash flow calculations. It also probably depends on the attitudes of preparers of accounts: many property investment companies were likely to welcome SSAP 19 because it reported their profits in a way which was more favourable, whereas many industrial companies were opposed to SSAP 16, possibly because it showed their profits in a less favourable light. Of course, it is unlikely that all preparers will be affected in the same way by a particular standard (e.g. some companies may wish to report lower, rather than higher, profits) and, from the reporting company's point of view, the best position is to have no standard at all, as in the case of fixed asset valuation, or a standard which allows many alternatives.

However, from the point of view of users of accounts, it seems likely that greater standardization of valuation principles is desirable, in order to facilitate the comparison of different reporting entities. For example, it is not clear that it is helpful for investment properties to be valued on a different basis from similar properties owned and occupied by members of the reporting group. It seems inevitable that the ASC, as a standard-setting body, will have to address the question of valuation on a more systematic basis. This may even occur during the current review of SSAP 2. Certainly if, as is possible, the ASC tries to develop some form of conceptual framework, giving greater clarity to the concept of economic substance on which it has relied in a number of instances, then it must certainly address the issue of valuation.

Together with the question of valuation, the ASC will have to consider the concept of capital maintenance, the necessary concomitant of valuation in measuring profit. The review of valuation problems in current accounting standards in the previous section referred to capital maintenance only in passing, because a full treatment of the subject in its own right would require a separate essay. Capital maintenance was, of course, a central issue in the debate on CCA (Whittington, 1984), and it underlies the current problems of reserve accounting.

No attempt has been made in this essay to discuss the precise form which the valuation base of company accounts might ideally take. This is a complex issue which has been debated thoroughly elsewhere. The broad stance adopted has been that some form of current valuation is likely to be more relevant to the needs of users of accounts than is historical cost, if we accept the view that users are concerned with the economic substance of the business at the time when the accounts are drawn up. The central message of the paper is that considerable departures from pure historical cost have already been made, that these are on an apparently haphazard basis, that there is a need for the ASC as the standard-setting body either to provide a systematic rationale for present practice or to standardize practice so that it can be made consistent with such a rationale. One type of model which could provide a systematic basis for accounting practice is price-change accounting, apparently abandoned when SSAP 16 ceased to be standard practice in 1985, but maintained and developed in the ASC's handbook, *Accounting for the Effects of Changing Prices* (1986).

REFERENCES

(a) Exposure drafts and standards

Accounting Standards Committee (ASC)

Exposure Drafts

ED 35	Accounting for the effects of changing prices (July, 1984)
ED 39	Accounting for pension costs (May, 1986)
ED 40	Stocks and long-term contracts (November, 1986)
ED 42	Accounting for special purpose transactions (March, 1988)

Standards

SSAP 2	Disclosure of accounting policies (November, 1971)
SSAP 9	Stocks and long-term contracts (May, 1975, revised September, 1988)
SSAP 12	Accounting for depreciation (originally issued December, 1977, amended November, 1981, revised January, 1987)
SSAP 14	Groups accounts (September, 1978)
SSAP 15	Accounting for deferred tax (October, 1978, revised May, 1985)
SSAP 19	Accounting for investment properties (November, 1981)
SSAP 20	Foreign currency translation (April, 1983)
SSAP 21	Accounting for leases and hire purchase contracts (August, 1984)
SSAP 23	Accounting for acquisitions and mergers (April, 1985)
SSAP 24	Accounting for pension costs (May, 1988)

Accounting Standards Steering Committee

Exposure Draft

ED 8   Accounting for changes in the purchasing power of money
            (January, 1973)

Standard

PSSAP 7   Accounting for changes in the purchasing power of money
            (May, 1974)

(b) Other references

ASC (1986) *Accounting for the Effects of Changing Prices: A Handbook,* ASC, London.

Bird, P. (1979) *Understanding Company Accounts,* Pitman, London.

Brindle, I. (1986) Off balance sheet financing, in *Financial Reporting 1985–86: A Survey of UK Published Accounts,* L.C.L. Skerratt and D.J. Tonkin (eds), Institute of Chartered Accountants in England and Wales, London.

Brindle, I. (1987) Off balance sheet financing, in *Financial Reporting 1986–87: A Survey of UK Reporting Practice,* L.C.L. Skerratt and D.J. Tonkin (eds), Institution of Chartered Accountants in England and Wales, London.

Griffiths, I. (1986) *Creative Accounting,* Sidgwick & Jackson, London.

Institute of Chartered Accountants in England and Wales (1987) *Accounting for Complex Capital Issues,* Technical Release 677, November.

Macdonald, N. (1987) Depreciation and revaluations of fixed assets, in *Financial Reporting 1986–87: A Survey of UK Reporting Practice,* L.C.L. Skerratt and D.J. Tonkin (eds), Institute of Chartered Accountants in England and Wales, London.

Sandilands, Report (1975) *Inflation Accounting,* Report of the Inflation Accounting Committee under the Chairmanship of F.E.P. Sandilands, Cmnd. 6225, HMSO, London.

HM Treasury Advisory Group (Chairman I.C.R. Byatt) (1986) *Accounting for Economic Costs and Changing Prices,* HMSO, London.

Tweedie, D.P. (1987) *Challenges Facing the Auditor: Professional Fouls and the Expectation Gap,* The Deloitte, Haskins & Sells Lecture, University College, Cardiff.

Tweedie, D.P. and Whittington G. (1984) *The Debate on Inflation Accounting,* Cambridge University Press, Cambridge.

Whittington, G. (1983) *Inflation Accounting: An Introduction to the Debate*, Cambridge University Press, Cambridge.

Whittington, G. (1984) Capital maintenance concepts in current cost accounting: recent developments in the United Kingdom, in *External Financial Reporting*, B. Carsberg and S. Dev (eds), Prentice-Hall, Englewood Cliffs, New Jersey.

Wild, K. (1987) Merger accounting and goodwill, in *Financial Reporting 1968–87: A Survey of UK Reporting Practice*, L.C.L. Skerratt and D.J. Tonkin (eds), Institute of Chartered Accountants in England and Wales, London.

11
Accounting for business combinations

ROBERT WILLOTT

INTRODUCTION

The accounting treatment applied to the combination of two or more businessess has long been a source of controversy, debate and conflicting practices. The choice of treatment adopted will determine whether or not pre-merger profits of both the combining entities remain available for distribution to the shareholders. Similarly, one accounting treatment will enable the consideration for the acquisition of another company to be shown at its 'fair' value whereas another treatment will enable the consideration to be shown at just the nominal value of the shares issued as the consideration.

For many years the accountancy profession and, to some extent, governments and other regulatory authorities have grappled with the need to arrive at a rational approach, an approach which not only reflects the substance of each transaction but at the same time achieves far greater consistency in presentation. This paper explores the background to current practices, reviews the distinctive characteristics of each practice and the problem areas which arise, and finally makes some specific suggestions about how business combinations might be accounted for in the future.

BACKGROUND

In August 1970 the Accounting Principles Board of the American

Institute of Certified Public Accountants pronounced on how the combining of two business entities should be reflected in US published financial statements. Prior to that, two alternative methods of accounting had been accepted in practice – the 'purchase' method and the 'pooling of interests' method (known in the United Kingdom as 'acquisition accounting' and 'merger accounting' respectively).

The Accounting Principles Board concluded that:

> . . . The purchase method and the pooling of interests method are both acceptable in accounting for business combinations, although *not as alternatives* in accounting for the same business combination. A business combination which meets specified conditions *requires* accounting by the pooling of interests method. A new basis of accounting is not permitted for a combination that meets the specified conditions, and the assets and liabilities of the combining companies are combined at their recorded amounts. All other business combinations should be accounted for as an acquisition of one or more companies by a corporation. The cost to an acquiring corporation of an entire acquired company should be determined by the principles of accounting for the acquisition of an asset. That cost should then be allocated to the identifiable individual assets acquired and liabilities assumed based on their fair values; the unallocated cost should be recorded as goodwill.
>
> (Opinion 16, para. 8, emphasis added.)

Under its constitution the Accounting Principles Board was required to obtain the support of two-thirds of its members for any Opinion it wished to issue. In 1970 the Board comprised 18 members (including its chairman). Just 12 of those members voted in favour of the Opinion on business combinations. In other words, the Opinion was adopted by the slenderest possible margin. The dissenting members were either totally opposed to the 'pooling of interests' (merger accounting) method in any form or wanted the method to be limited to the very rare circumstances where, in addition to fulfilling the criteria specified in the Opinion, the combining businesses were of relative sizes which would indicate a significant sharing of ownership risks and benefits.

Against this backcloth of rather fragile US support for merger accounting, the United Kingdom accountancy bodies set to work to establish an acceptable Statement of Standard Accounting Practice for promulgation here. The result (SSAP 23) emerged in April 1985 with the title *Accounting for Acquisitions and Mergers.*

Prior to the issue of the UK accounting standard, domestic practices had been influenced (and, some might say, impaired) by an uncertain legal regime which had discouraged merger accounting. However, those legal inhibitions were removed by the Companies Act 1981 (now s. 131, Companies Act 1985). It then became possible for the UK accounting standard to follow the US precedent and in broad terms that is what happened. Indeed the UK accounting standard embraced merger accounting with considerably more enthusiasm than was evident in the US Opinion some 15 years earlier and offered a more flexible approach in its application.

The UK accounting standard allows companies to adopt merger accounting at their option if all of the following conditions are met (para. 11, SSAP 23):

1. The business combination results from an offer to the holders of all equity shares and the holders of all voting shares which are not already held by the offerer; and
2. The offerer has secured, as a result of the offer, a holding of (a) at least 90% of all equity shares (taking each class of equity separately), and (b) shares carrying at least 90% of the votes of the offeree; and
3. Immediately prior to the offer, the offerer does not hold (a) 20% or more of all equity shares of the offeree (taking each class of equity shares separately), or (b) shares carrying 20% or more of the votes of the offeree; and
4. Not less than 90% of the fair value of the total consideration given for the equity share capital (including that given for shares already held) is in the form of equity share capital and not less than 90% of the fair value of the total consideration given for voting non-equity share capital (including that given for shares already held) is in the form of equity and/or voting non-equity share capital.

If a business combination does not meet all the conditions set out above, it must be accounted for as an acquisition. Thus acquisition accounting may be applied in any circumstances whereas merger accounting is available only in limited circumstances and then entirely at the company's option. This optional approach contrasts with the prescriptive nature of the US Opinion, but that is not the only way in which the UK accounting standard is more flexible than its US counterpart.

There is really only one test which has to be met if a UK company wishes to adopt merger accounting and that, put simply, is: has the business combination been achieved by means of a share exchange? By contrast the US Opinion recognizes that a different accounting practice cannot be justified simply on the basis of whether the consideration is in shares or in cash. The essence of a business combination which qualifies for merger accounting in the US is the clear intention that the combining entities will continue as independent units and their respective shareholders will continue as owners of the combined businesses. Nevertheless the actual criteria specified in the US Opinion are less precise than they might be – see the Canadian approach, for example (*Canadian Institute of Chartered Accountants Handbook*, section 1580) – requiring merger accounting if but only if (paragraphs 46–8):

1. Each of the combining companies is autonomous and has not been a subsidiary or division of another corporation within two years before the plan of combination is initiated.
2. Each of the combining companies is independent of the other combining companies.
3. The combination is effected in a single transaction or is completed in accordance with a specific plan within one year after the plan is initiated.
4. A corporation offers and issues only common stock with rights identical to those of the majority of its outstanding voting common stock in exchange for substantially all (generally 90%) of the voting common stock interest of another company at the date the plan of combination is consummated.
5. None of the combining companies changes the equity interest of the voting common stock in contemplation of effecting the combination either within two years before the plan of combin-

ation is initiated or between the dates the combination is initiated and consummated; changes in contemplation of effecting the combination may include distributions to stockholders and additional issuances, exchanges and retirements of securities.

6. Each of the combining companies re-acquires shares of voting common stock only for purposes other than business combinations, and no company re-acquires more than a normal number of shares between the dates the plan of combination is initiated and consummated.

7. The ratio of the interest of an individual common stockholder to those of other common stockholders in a combining company remains the same as a result of the exchange of stock to effect the combination.

8. The voting rights to which the common stock ownership interests in the resulting combined corporation are entitled are exercisable by the stockholders; the stockholders are neither deprived of nor restricted in exercising those rights for a period.

9. The combination is resolved at the date the plan is consummated and no provisions of the plan relating to the issue of securities or other considerations are pending.

10. The combined corporation does not agree directly or indirectly to retire or re-acquire all or part of the common stock issued to effect the combination.

11. The combined corporation does not enter into other financial arrangements for the benefit of the former stockholders of a combining company, such as a guarantee of loans secured by stock issued in the combination, which in effect negates the exchange of equity securities.

12. The combined corporation does not intend or plan to dispose of a significant part of the assets of the combining companies within two years after the combination other than disposals in the ordinary course of business of the formerly separate companies and to eliminate duplicate facilities or excess capacity.

The background picture would be incomplete without also taking into account the European Communities Seventh Company Law

Directive. This Directive requires the UK government to introduce legislation governing the preparation of consolidated accounts for groups of companies. Such legislation could include provisions which would have the effect of either requiring or permitting merger accounting in circumstances to be specified. The appropriate legislation is already overdue and there has been a continuing dialogue between the Department of Trade and Industry and the accountancy profession aimed at achieving the most satisfactory outcome. At the time of writing, the Department favours:

1. *Permitting but not requiring* merger accounting in circumstances broadly compatible with those specified in the UK accounting standard;
2. *Requiring* acquisition accounting in all circumstances where companies do not take advantage of the option in (1) above;
3. Requiring additional disclosure;
4. Harmonizing existing company law with the Directive in specifying when an investment in a subsidiary company may be included at the nominal value of the shares issued as consideration (thereby avoiding recognition of any share premium).

The Directive clearly would give the UK government an opportunity to adopt a far more restrictive approach to the use of merger accounting as well as to outlaw some of the perceived abuses. Whether that would be desirable or whether the Accounting Standards Committee is better placed to deal with such matters is the subject of continuing debate.

THE ACCOUNTING METHODS EXPLAINED

What are the characteristics of acquisition accounting and merger accounting? How do they differ and why?

The principal characteristics of acquisition accounting are as follows:

1. The *cost of acquiring the new subsidiary* is recorded at its '*fair*' *value* – that means the cash outlay and/or the current value of any shares issued as part of the consideration (in the case of a public company the market price of the shares issued at the date

of the transaction will often be used in arriving at the fair value of the consideration).

2. The *underlying net assets of the newly acquired subsidiary are individually revalued* at the date of acquisition and any remaining shortfall between the revalued net assets and the cost of acquisition is recorded in the consolidated accounts as 'goodwill'. (If the revalued net assets exceed the cost of acquisition, the surplus is credited to reserves.)

3. *Pre-acquisition profits* of the subsidiary are *excluded* from the amount of consolidated profits shown in the profit and loss account as available for distribution to shareholders of the parent company.

By contrast, merger accounting has the following features:

1. The *cost of acquisition* is recorded at the *nominal value* of the shares issued by the 'acquiring' company together with the amount of any cash element included in the consideration. (Note that merger accounting would not be permissible if a significant cash element is included in the consideration.)

2. Assets and liabilities of the two entities are combined at their existing book values *without revaluation.*

3. *Pre-merger profits* and other reserves are combined in the consolidated balance sheet – pre-merger profits *remain distributable* to the continuing shareholders.

4. The *consolidated profit and loss* account includes the combined profits of both entities for the full extent of the accounting period in which the merger occurs (as well as in the revised comparative figures for the previous year).

To illustrate the main differences between acquisition accounting and merger accounting, let us assume that a company called Topco plc purchases all the share capital of Subsidiary Ltd. The balance sheets of the two companies at the date of combination might look like this:

	Topco		Subsidiary	
Fixed assets:	£	£	£	£
Plant and machinery		6000		1200
Investment – Subsidiary Ltd		4000		—
Current assets	3500	10000	800	1200
Current liabilities	3000	500	500	300
Net assets		£10500		£1500
Represented by:				
Share capital		2500		1000
Share premium		3250		—
Retained profits		4750		500
		£10500		£1500

The consolidated balance sheet would appear as follows, depending on whether acquisition accounting or merger accounting is adopted:

	Acquisition accounting		Merger accounting	
Fixed assets:	£	£	£	£
Plant and machinery (note)		8500		7200
Goodwill on consolidation		1200		—
		9700		7200
Current assets	4300		4300	
Current liabilities	3500	800	3500	800
Net assets		£10500		£8000
Represented by:				
Share capital		2500		2500
Share premium		3250		—
Consolidation adjustment				250
		5750		2750
Retained profits		4750		5250
		£10500		£8000

Note: Plant and machinery has been revalued upwards by £1300 in accordance with acquisition accounting principles.

In the above example, the most obvious differences in presentation are:

1. *Fixed assets* are greater under acquisition accounting than under merger accounting (reflecting the requirement to revalue the net assets where acquisition accounting is adopted) and consequently future depreciation charges will also increase.

2. *Goodwill* arises under acquisition accounting (being the excess of the fair value of the consideration over the fair value of net assets acquired) and to comply with UK accounting standards (SSAP 22, *Accounting for Goodwill*) this item must be amortized in the consolidated profit and loss account or written off at inception.

3. *Share premium* arises under acquisition accounting, reflecting the full ('fair') value of the shares issued as consideration for the acquisition of Subsidiary Ltd, whereas under merger accounting only the nominal value of the new shares has to be reflected in the balance sheet. (Note that if certain company law criteria are met it may be possible to redesignate the share premium as a 'merger reserve' which in turn may be used to absorb goodwill arising on consolidation – the detailed merger relief provisions are discussed later in this paper.)

4. *Retained profits* are greater under merger accounting than under acquisition accounting because merger accounting allows the cumulative profits of both the combining entities to remain available to shareholders (on the grounds that all predecessor shareholders are in theory both able and willing to retain their investment in the combining group).

It should also be noted that the calculation of 'earnings per share' will produce different figures depending on the accounting method adopted. Not only will the earnings for the first accounting period be lower under acquisition accounting (because pre-acquisition profits of Subsidiary Ltd. must be excluded) but also the average number of shares in issue will be lower.

So far we have examined the presentational differences between acquisition accounting and merger accounting and the circumstances in which merger accounting may be used instead of acquisition accounting. Yet we have avoided addressing the fundamental question of whether in reality there are any clearly identifiable difference of substance between what is called a 'merger' and what is called an 'acquisition'. And, even if such differences could be identified, do they legitimately justify the adoption of substantially different accounting practices?

The impression gained from most so-called 'mergers' is that they are no such thing. Commonly one company identifies a target, makes an approach and (with a little skill and a bigger portion of good luck) secures agreement to its offer to 'merge'. Once the transaction is completed the predator takes command of all or most strategic management positions. As to whether a share exchange, rather than a cash consideration, reflects any special conceptual characteristics attaching to the transaction, the truthful answer would usually be 'no'. Shares are offered when the offerer believes that these will be more appealing to the offerees or when there may be specific financial benefits accruing to the offerer by doing so. Of course there will always be the exceptional case where the parties would be able to demonstrate that their combination genuinely arose from mutual aspirations and genuinely reflected a desire by both parties to share in the combined risks and rewards of their respective entities. But even in those rare cases there appears to be sufficient disagreement among the professionals to justify far more caution before permitting the practices of merger accounting.

It seems likely that most advocates of merger accounting do so for its financial and/or presentational benefits rather than from any desire to portray a conceptually fairer view of the substance of the transaction. If this is so, the issue to be addressed goes beyond conceptual niceties and challenges the credibility of any financial statement which adopts merger accounting principles.

THE PROBLEMS WITH MERGER ACCOUNTING

To appreciate why merger accounting leads to abuse it is instructive to examine some of the problem areas in greater detail. The examples are by no means exhaustive.

1. *Non-comparability.* Whilst the current level of flexibility remains, an entity may account for one business combination as

a merger and the next combination as an acquisition. Yet in practice the two transactions may be identical in every respect except that one involved only a share exchange whereas the other included perhaps a modest cash element. Worse still, both transactions could be identical and the difference in presentation could simply result from management choice. (Of choice, lack of comparability also affects judgements between companies.)

2. *Vendor placings.* Here a company is enabled to present as a merger a transaction which is nothing more than a cash purchase. All the acquiring company has to do is to arrange for the vendor shareholders to contract with a securities firm for the placing of the shares they receive as consideration for the disposal of their interest in the target company. Thus a cash purchase is made to look like a share exchange, for a few days anyway.

3. *Profiting from other people's gains.* Because merger accounting does not require the revaluation of assets at the time of the combination, unrealized gains may be converted into cash profits by subsequent disposal of the assets concerned and those profits may be included in post-acquisition income. (Disclosure of such windfall profits is required by the Companies Act 1985 (Sched. 4, para. 75), but some argue that disclosure is no substitute for a fairer computation of profit.)

4. *Understanding the cost of the target company.* By including the share-for-share consideration at the nominal value of the new shares issued, the issuing company may benefit in at least two ways. First, future profits from the investment will *not* be measured against the market value of consideration given (contrast that with the situation where the transaction is financed by a rights issue). And secondly, there will be no need to create goodwill to reflect any excess of consideration over the fair value of the net assets required (and, consequently, no need to find a way to write off that goodwill without impacting on annual profits).

5. *Improving and/or distorting earnings per share.* When using merger accounting it is assumed that the enlarged share capital has been in existence for all time and the earnings of the combining companies are also treated in this way. By

comparison, under acquisition accounting the earnings of the acquired company are included only from the date of acquisition and the number of shares in issue for the year is calculated by adjusting the year-end position to reflect the timing and amount of additional issues during the year. It follows that seasonal fluctuations in profits and other adjustments made by the management will materially distort the earnings per share when merger accounting is used. The desire to maximize earnings per share is a strong influence on many of the companies which opt for merger accounting.

From the above it will be clear that there is a strong incentive for companies to use merger accounting not because of any inherent merit but simply because it enables them to present a better picture of performance by avoiding the unwelcome consequences of acquisition accounting. It is therefore appropriate to examine further some of those unwelcome consequences, to consider whether they are desirable nevertheless or, if they are not desirable, to consider whether they are avoidable without recourse to merger accounting.

THE UNWELCOME FEATURES OF ACQUISITION ACCOUNTING

The most commonly cited objections to acquisition accounting include:

1. The creation and consequent amortization/write-off of goodwill (especially among 'people businesses') plus the added complication of deferred/contingent consideration;
2. Increases in depreciation charges arising from upward revaluation of fixed assets where applicable;
3. Perceived constraints on the distribution of 'pre-acquisition' profits;
4. Difficulties in establishing the appropriate 'date of acquisition' and carrying out the necessary accounting adjustments and revaluations at that date.

Without doubt the goodwill implications loom prominently in the minds of many companies, especially those 'people businesses' which have little in the way of tangible fixed assets. There are two questions to address here. First, is it appropriate to recognize the fair value of the company being acquired? And if it is, what is the best way of dealing with goodwill when it arises?

It is hard to accept that the price paid for another company should be recorded at a different amount simply because of the method used to pay for it. Even if a case could be argued for adopting a different method of accounting on those rare occasions where a business combination truly reflects a bringing together of two businesses and their shareholders on a continuing basis, there is an urgent need to standardize the method of valuing the target company in all other circumstances. Indeed it could be argued that *all* business combinations should be recorded by attributing a fair value to the new shares issued as consideration. The choice of consideration between cash, loan stock or shares should not normally affect the value attributed to the target company. And if it was not for the problem of goodwill, it seems most unlikely that many companies would give a second thought to the use of merger accounting.

So is there a way of overcoming the goodwill problem? Clearly, if the fair value paid for a company exceeds the fair value of the net assets acquired, the excess has to be reflected in the accounts somewhere. As already indicated, the UK accounting standard (SSAP 22) encourages companies to write off goodwill immediately it arises by a direct charge against reserves. As a less favoured alternative, companies may amortize the goodwill over its economic life. Given a choice most companies would prefer to write off the goodwill at the outset because this avoids an annual charge against profits and earnings per share. The difficulty arises when there are no reserves available to absorb the write-off, but three ways round this obstacle have now emerged.

The first way to overcome a shortage of reserves is to take advantage of the 'merger relief' provisions contained in the Companies Act 1985 (ss. 131 *et seq.*). These provisions were introduced in 1981 principally to overcome the legal obstacles to merger accounting at that time by excusing the issuing company from creating a share premium account in specified circumstances.

However, the relief brought in by the new legislation extends beyond situations where merger accounting would be permitted even under the flexible framework of the current UK accounting standard. In general terms merger relief is available wherever the purchase consideration is in equity shares issued at a price which would usually give rise to the creation of a share premium and:

1. In pursuance of the purchase arrangement the issuing company have secured at least a 90% equity holding in the other company;
2. The consideration for the shares issued by the investing company is either equity shares in the other company or the cancellation of any such equity shares not already held by the investing company.

Merger relief is available in the above circumstances even where the issuing company already holds a substantial proportion of the other company's equity shares (although naturally the relief applies only to shares issued as part of the arrangement which secures the 90% investment, and not to shares issued previously). It does not matter if, as part of the qualifying arrangement, some shares are purchased for cash but to the extent that shares are purchased for cash rather than in exchange for shares the amount available for merger relief will be correspondingly reduced. Relief also extends to any shares issued in exchange for non-equity shares as part of the overall arrangement whereby the 90% equity holding is acquired. It is not even necessary for the 'arrangement' to be limited to a single transaction or to transactions at a single point in time. The arrangement may include subsequent issues of equity shares to satisfy deferred consideration. The only requirement is that all the transactions are contained within the one 'arrangement'. Thus the merger relief provisions enable many companies to treat as 'reserves' the amounts which would otherwise have been capitalized as 'share premium'. Against those reserves may be set the goodwill arising on consolidating the financial statements with the acquired company with those of the acquiring company. In most businesses it is common for the value of goodwill to equate broadly with the merger reserves arising from the issue of the consideration shares.

The second method of overcoming the need to amortize goodwill against profits is to create what is inelegantly called the 'dangling debit'. This involves presenting the goodwill item as a deduction from reserves and thereby reducing the aggregate amount of share-holders' funds. Many companies are now describing the debit as a 'reserve' which must be the most flagrant abuse of the term ever devised. Indeed the term 'merger reserve' is used by some companies to describe the amount created by applying the merger relief provisions to the issue of new shares and by other companies to describe the dangling debit.

The third method is simply a variation of the other two. By applying to the courts it may be possible to convert an existing share premium into other reserves. The applicant will need to demonstrate that the interests of creditors will not be prejudiced by what is deemed to be a reduction of permanent capital. Once the court is satisfied the company will hopefully have sufficient reserves available against which to offset goodwill, even goodwill previously shown as a dangling debit!

Whatever people may think of the methods involved, at present there is a fair amount of scope for companies to write off goodwill against reserves without the need to make annual charges against profits and earnings per share. Therefore it is hardly surprising that on the introduction of the accounting standard governing goodwill many companies opted for, or switched to, an immediate write-off policy.* Whether this policy will be allowed to continue is another matter. It is known that the Accounting Standards Committee is reviewing the standard on goodwill and a growing body of opinion would seem to be in favour of making the amortization route the rule rather than the exception. This would put the UK on a similar basis as the US where amortization is mandatory.

However, there is a danger in requiring all companies to amortize goodwill against annual profits, despite the resultant improvement in comparability of financial reporting. It would be particularly contentious to impose such a requirement on companies whose main asset is people. Indeed there are arguments for treating 'people busi-

*For example, in the annual survey of financial results of advertising agencies compiled by Spicer & Oppenheim, the number of companies adopting the immediate write-off method more than doubled between the 1985 sample and the 1986 sample, and this trend continued in each subsequent period.

nesses' differently from those with a substantial 'tangible asset' base. Those arguments include:

1. The replacement of a 'people' asset (to which the goodwill value broadly relates) does not consume capital resources of the entity. Instead all costs of replacement, enhancement and maintenance are charged in the profit and loss account by way of labour costs as they are incurred. Provided the people resource is properly managed and replaced where appropriate, the earning capacity will be maintained. If not, earnings will decline. By contrast, as tangible fixed assets depreciate, they must be replaced out of capital. Consequently, if a case could be made that goodwill arising on the acquisition of an entity which depends on tangible fixed assets for the maintenance of the operation should be amortized in a manner broadly comparable to the policy applied to those underlying tangible fixed assets, there would be an equally strong argument against amortizing goodwill associated with any intangible assets which do not consume capital.

2. Goodwill traditionally has been regarded as a premium paid in excess of the net tangible assets acquired to reflect the 'super profits' being generated – that is, a return on net assets above what might be regarded as a fairly standard return. In such circumstances it has been argued that the premium should be amortized against those profits. In a people business, the price a purchaser might pay to obtain merely a 'reasonable' level of return would far exceed the net tangible assets acquired. To amortize that excess element of the acquisition cost would seem somewhat illogical. To distinguish between that 'basic' cost and any price for 'super profits' would be highly subjective at best and meaningless at worst.

3. In a people business, the useful economic life of purchased goodwill is impossible to assess. It bears no resemblance to, for example, the remaining useful working lives of key personnel because they can be replaced without further capital outlay. Equally, it is impossible for an auditor to judge the value of an individual's contribution to a company's earning capacity. Thus there is great scope for directors to insist on entirely subjective amortization periods, which may vary between companies and be inconsistent with economic reality in a particular case.

Whether it would be practicable to impose one set of rules for people businesses and another set of rules for those which have a significant dependence on tangible fixed assets must be an open question. Certainly an immediate write-off against reserves in both circumstances provides a prudent compromise. Irrespective of the ideal answer, the existing accounting standard must surely be deficient in that it allows choice without adequate disclosure of what the effect of adopting the alternative treatment would have been.

At the very least, there should be a requirement to state the gross amount of shareholders' funds prior to any reduction arising from writing off goodwill directly against reserves, as well as the aggregate amount of such goodwill write-offs to date. In addition, where the immediate write-off route is adopted, the notional effect on earnings per share of amortizing goodwill against profits over a specified period of 20 or 40 years should be stated on the face of the profit and loss account.

The situation becomes even more complicated where the target company is acquired on terms which include an element of deferred or contingent consideration – what is now commonly known as an 'earn-out'. Where the deferred element is a defined sum, best practice is to include it as part of the overall purchase price thereby increasing any goodwill arising. If the purchase consideration is to be in shares, they will not have been issued at the time the goodwill is recognized. Consequently the goodwill may be too great to be absorbed by existing reserves without the benefit of the proceeds of the new share issue and the application of merger relief. Where the deferred consideration is contingent on the achievement of certain profit targets, it is almost impossible to arrive at a meaningful estimate of the likely future payment. For this reason most companies omit any such estimate both from the cost of acquisition initially recorded in the balance sheet and from the initial calcu-lation of goodwill arising on consolidation, resorting instead to a simple note of the contingent liability. A discussion paper issued by the Accounting Standards Committee in the early part of 1988 advocates that companies should place a value on any contingent purchase consideration. If this view gains support the biggest item in the accounts of acquisitive 'people' businesses will be a meaningless guesstimate of the goodwill element. In many cases, to comply with prevailing accounting standards the only practicable accounting treatment would be to amortize that guesstimate against profits and earnings per share, adjusting the amount when the eventual liability is ascertained. Certainly, available reserves will often be insufficient to absorb an immediate write-off of goodwill arising from an estimated liability as yet uncrystallized.

Enough has been written here and elsewhere to demonstrate that goodwill arising on an acquisition causes considerable difficulties and that those difficulties are sufficient to encourage the use of merger accounting wherever possible. There is less evidence to suggest that many companies are unhappy about the increased depreciation charges which flow from any upward revaluation of fixed assets at the date of the amalgamation. Of course, as the balancing figure between the revalued net assets and the purchase consideration will be goodwill (or possibly a capital reserve) a company which takes a cautious view when revaluing its assets may be faced with amortizing a correspondingly higher amount of goodwill against profits. Either way earnings per share would suffer.

By comparison it may be thought that investing companies are less worried about being deprived of access to the pre-acquisition profits of investee companies. At present acquisition accounting requires pre-acquisition reserves to be 'frozen' in the consolidated accounts at the time of acquisition. Thus the combined entities will include only the post-acquisition profits of the investee company as part of the group's retained profits. By implication pre-acquisition profits of the investee company are not distributable to shareholders in the investor company, although there is nothing to prohibit the investee company from paying dividends up to the investor company out of pre-acquisition profits. However, such dividends are deducted from the original cost of investment and as a consequence both the cost of acquisition and the amount attributable to the net assets acquired are correspondingly reduced. Therefore the payment of the dividend does not increase the group's profits available for distribution.

By contrast merger accounting recognizes that, where the shareholders of two separate entities combine to become co-owners of the merged businesses, the combination should not of itself restrict the continuing availability to those shareholders of the profits earned during their ownership of the separate entities. The retained profits of both companies are amalgamated and remain distributable.

There is little recent evidence that companies effecting a combination by share exchange have elected to use merger accounting principally to preserve access to pre-merger profits of the investee company, but no doubt it is one of the factors which is taken into consideration. In isolated cases it may prove to be critical, but generally the parties will be more concerned about ensuring that *future* earnings per share show an improvement over the pre-merger performance.

In any case, it would be relatively simple to introduce a facility within acquisition accounting which enabled pre-acquisition profits of the investee company to be distributed where the combination is effected by share exchange (see Willott (1983)). The accounting standard would merely have to recognize that, in those circumstances where a company is acquired by share exchange and virtually all its previous shareholders are given the opportunity to continue as shareholders in the acquiring company, the continuing interest of those shareholders would be reflected by creating a merger revaluation reserve (using the merger relief provisions of the Companies Act) instead of a share premium. That reserve would be distributable to the extent that it is realized and it would be regarded as realized only when, and to the extent that, the pre-merger reserves of the new subsidiary are distributed to the investing company. In the investing company's accounts the carrying value of the investment (which in reality is comprised of the investment in the nominal value of the share capital of the subsidiary plus cumulative pre-merger reserves, namely retained profits, surpluses arising on revaluing assets at the date of the acquisition and the value placed on goodwill at the date of acquisition) would be reduced by the amount of any dividend received from the subsidiary. At the same time a transfer would be made from the merger revaluation reserve to distributable reserves in the balance sheet of the investing company.

The third of the above-mentioned problem areas with acquisition accounting – establishing the appropriate date of acquisition and carrying out the necessary adjustments and asset revaluations at that date – cannot be regarded as a valid objection to the accounting method as such. Nevertheless, it can create considerable extra work. It may also give rise to controversy. The controversial aspect concerns the date of acquisition. According to accounting standards the effective date of acquisition of a subsidiary is 'the earlier of (a) the date on which consideration passes, or (b) the date on which an offer becomes or is declared unconditional' (SSAP 14, *Group Accounts*, para. 32). And when legislation was introduced to specify the matters to be disclosed when merger relief is adopted, the effective date to be used for identifying any profits or losses of the newly acquired subsidiary which have arisen prior to the arrangement but which have been included in the group accounts of the combining companies (which in many cases would coincide with the date of acquisition of a subsidiary) was defined as:

1. The date on which the investing company obtains more than half in nominal value of the investee company's equity share capital, or
2. The date on which the investing company, being a member of the investee company, gains control of the composition of the investee company's board of directors,

with the proviso that, where the arrangement by which the investee company becomes a subsidiary company is binding only upon fulfilment of a condition, the effective date will be that on which the condition is fulfilled. (This is a simplified definition drawn from the Companies Act 1985, Sched. 4, para. 75 (4), read in conjunction with s. 736.) Thus the law avoids any specific reference to the passing of consideration as the effective date although in most cases the date of acquisition of the shares will coincide with the passing of consideration.

But the timing problem rarely revolves around the minor differences between the definition found in the accounting standard and the one used in legislation. The real difficulty arises when an acquiring company seeks to bring into its accounts the results of an acquired company from a date *before* that prescribed in either the law or the accounting standard. The situation is exacerbated when the parties to the amalgamation are not prepared to carry out the necessary accounting and valuation work on the effective acquisition date. For example, stocks and work in progress may need to be assessed fairly precisely. It is not unknown for companies simply to use management accounting figures made up to the nearest convenient date or to argue for time apportionment of profits or losses without regard to seasonal or other actual distortions.

Although merger accounting also requires profits to be allocated between those earned before the merger and those earned afterwards, the information has only to be shown in the notes and therefore tends to be treated less seriously. Furthermore, there is no requirement to revalue the assets at all.

A WAY FORWARD

If there were an obviously simpler and better alternative method of accounting for business combinations, presumably that method would already be adopted. Yet surely it must be acknowledged that the present arrangements are far from ideal and deserve a more fundamental reappraisal than they have received so far. What conclusions flow from the matters addressed in this review?

1. The principles of merger accounting as currently practised have insufficient support on either side of the Atlantic to justify its adoption as either a mandatory or an optional standard accounting practice.
2. Those who elect to use merger accounting in the UK are less likely to be influenced by any theoretical justification and more likely to be motivated by a desire to present a better financial position than would otherwise be the case.
3. Unless the combination is accounted for in a manner which reflects the fair value of any consideration given, it is impossible to assess fairly the future financial benefits of the transaction.
4. An inevitable consequence of reflecting the consideration at fair value will be the creation of goodwill on consolidation of the combining companies' financial statements and a need to arrive at a more rational policy for dealing with this intangible asset.
5. If merger accounting were to be outlawed, it would be necessary explicitly to permit companies which effect a combination by share exchange to continue to distribute pre-combination profits to shareholders subject to the need to avoid prejudicing the interests of creditors.

The adoption of a single method of accounting for business combinations which involved the adoption of fair values, the continuing distributability of pre-combination profits where shareholders of both entities are able to retain their investment, and a sensible policy for dealing with goodwill, would overcome many of the abuses and introduce far greater comparability. Can it be done?

Here, as a basis for further discussion, is a suggested outline of a new accounting standard, also incorporating some features of goodwill accounting:

Definitions

1.1 A 'business combination' arises when one or more companies become subsidiaries of another company except in circumstances constituting a group reorganization as defined below.

1.2 A 'group reorganization' means either a combining of one or more companies as subsidiaries of another company pursuant to a group reconstruction defined in s. 132 of the Companies Act 1985 or any other similar combining of two or more companies which are already under common control. 'Common control' means that one or more persons between them hold not less than (say) 90% of the equity capital of each company.

Method of accounting

2.1 All business combinations should be accounted for as acquisitions.

2.2 Group reorganizations may be accounted for as mergers.

Acquisition accounting

3.1 Where a business combination is accounted for as an acquisition, the fair value of the purchase consideration should, for the purposes of consolidated financial statements, be allocated between the underlying net tangible and intangible assets other than goodwill, on the basis of the fair value to the acquiring company in accordance with SSAP 14, *Group Accounts*. Any difference between the fair value of the consideration and the aggregate of the fair values of the separable net assets including identifiable intangibles such as patents, licences and trademarks will represent goodwill which should be accounted for in accordance with paragraph 3.2 below.

3.2 Goodwill arising on consolidation should be written off immediately against reserves or, if retained as an asset, should be shown as a deduction from shareholders' funds. Where goodwill is written off, the balance sheet or notes thereto should show (a) the gross amount of reserves before deduction of the aggregate amount of goodwill so written off to date, and (b) the aggregate amount of goodwill written off against reserves to date. Companies to which SSAP 3, *Earnings per Share* applied should also state what effect there would be on earnings per share if goodwill were to be amortized against profits over a period of (say) 20 years.

3.3 Where a business combination is effected by an issue of equity shares of the investing company in exchange for equity shares of the investee company, and as a result the issuing company secures a holding of at least 90% of all equity shares (taking each class separately) of the investee company, the excess of the fair value of the consideration shares over the nominal value of those shares should be included in the balance sheet as a 'merger reserve' and not as a share premium (taking advantage of s. 131 of the Companies Act 1985).

3.4 To the extent that it is not otherwise applied and subject to the requirements of company law, a merger reserve arising in accordance with paragraph 3.3 above may be distributed to shareholders when, and to the extent that, any pre-combination profits of the new subsidiary are distributed to the investing company.

3.5 Dividends received by the investing company out of pre-combination profits of the investee company should be applied to reduce the carrying value of the investment in the financial statements of the investing company.

3.6 The results of the investee company should be included in the consolidated financial statements from the effective date of the business combination (as defined) only.

Merger accounting

4.1 In those group reorganizations where merger accounting is applied, it is not necessary to adjust the carrying values of the assets and liabilities of the subsidiary to fair value either in its own books or on consolidation. However, appropriate adjustments should be made to achieve uniformity of accounting policies between the combining companies.

4.2 Where consolidated financial statements are prepared for the companies involved in the group reorganization, a difference may arise between the carrying value of the investment in a subsidiary (which will be the nominal value of the shares issued as consideration plus the fair value of any additional consideration) and the nominal value of the shares transferred to the issuing company. Where the carrying value of the investment is less than the nominal value of the shares transferred, the difference should be treated as a reserve on consolidation. Where the carrying value of the investment is greater than the nominal value of the shares transferred, the difference is the extent to which reserves have been in effect capitalized as a result of the reorganization and it should therefore be treated on consolidation as a reduction of reserves.

4.3 Where consolidated financial statements are prepared for those companies involved in the group reorganization, the profits or losses of subsidiaries brought in for the first time should be included for the entire accounting period during which the reorganization takes place without adjustment to exclude the results for that part of the period prior to the reorganization. Corresponding amounts should be presented as if the companies had been part of the reorganized group throughout the previous period and at the previous balance sheet date.

The application of merger accounting principles to group reorganizations will depend to some extent on the nature of the reorganization and further consideration may have to be given to this aspect. However, it is little more than a side issue to the main issue of how to account for business combinations generally.

The above outline standard does not deal comprehensively with disclosure matters which would need to incorporate existing statutory requirements and best practice.

As the Accounting Standards Committee reviews its current requirements affecting acquisitions and mergers, perhaps this analysis will make a constructive contribution to that debate.

REFERENCES

Accounting Standards Committee (1988) *Fair Value in the Context of Acquisition Accounting: A Discussion Paper,* Institute of Chartered Accountants in England and Wales, London.

Willott, R. (1983) Has ED 31 got it right? 94 : 1077, 133–5. *Accountancy,* May.

12

The regulation of privately owned utilities: an accounting challenge

BRYAN CARSBERG

The United Kingdom has recently adopted a new package of measures for promoting efficiency in the national utilities. I am responsible for regulation in the telecommunications industry and this has a number of features in common with the arrangements already implemented for gas and currently proposed for electricity and water. A key step in the package of measures is to transfer ownership from the state to the private sector of the economy. A second key element is to introduce competition in a number of areas which were previously regarded as appropriate for monopoly supply. And the third main measure is to establish independent regulation.

It would perhaps be too strong to claim that the job of regulator was tailor-made for an accountant but the job certainly does raise a number of interesting and complex issues for accountants. I shall discuss some examples of these accounting issues in this paper. The subject is an apt one for a book of essays in memory of Peter Bird because the issues are related to the general questions of how to obtain good accountability and this was a topic about which Peter thought and wrote a good deal.

THE REGULATORY FRAMEWORK

My Office – The Office of Telecommunications (OFTEL) – was created under the Telecommunications Act 1984. This Act gives me the duty of promoting the interests of users of telecommunications services as regards price, quality and variety of services. It also gives me the duty of promoting competition in the industry – competition that was established to some extent earlier under the Telecommunications Act 1981 – and of promoting efficiency in the industry. Evidently, the concept underlying the Act is that competition is frequently the best way of promoting the interests of users because it tends to ensure that products and services are supplied efficiently and that innovative services are produced as soon as possible. A firm that is not sufficiently efficient is unlikely to survive in a competitive market and firms facing competition – unlike monopolists – cannot take a relaxed attitude towards the introduction of innovative services for fear that a competitor will beat them to the introduction of those services and win their customers away.

The Act also establishes the framework within which I must fulfil my duties. It states that telecommunications services can be provided only by companies which have licences to do so. The licences are to be issued by the Secretary of State for Trade and Industry but he has the obligation of considering my advice before deciding whether or not to issue them. The licences contain rules which set down the extent of permitted competition and they also require compliance with rules of fair trading, without which competition might prove to be impossible. I have the duty of enforcing the licence rules and, if I think that additional rules are needed, I can initiate procedures for making an amendment to the rules and subsequently make the amendment: if the change in rules is disputed by the licensee, I have to obtain the broad support of the Monopolies and Mergers Commission before I can make the amendment. Thus, I can use my functions of enforcing licence rules, seeking amendments to those rules, and advising the Secretary of State about the issuing of new licences to promote competition in the interests of the users of telecommunications products and services.

THE PROMOTION OF COMPETITION

The pivotal issue that arises in the promotion of competition is in the decision about how much competition is desirable. The position that prevailed when OFTEL was established was that the government had instituted a duopoly policy for the supply of basic telecommunications services. British Telecom was the long-established monopoly supplier of telecommunications services in all parts of the country except Hull where a separate telephone system was operated by the local authority. The government had licensed Mercury Communications as a second operator, to compete with British Telecom and the Hull network, giving it the obligation to build a network of a specified minimum size but with freedom to go much further. Mercury was obliged, in effect, to provide services over many of the major trunk routes but it was not obliged to serve the minor trunk routes and it also had a choice about whether or not to build local networks, comprising local exchanges and links between the local exchanges and customers' premises and trunk exchanges.

The government also adopted a policy of licensing cable television companies and these companies are being permitted to provide competing local telecommunications networks on two conditions: they must provide the telecommunications services under an agreement with BT or Mercury – for example, on the basis that BT or Mercury would provide local switching for the calls which would be collected and/or delivered over the cable television company's network – and provided that the cable television company has obtained a determination from me declaring that a reasonable demand exists for the telecommunications services it will provide. In carrying out my duty to promote competition, therefore, I have to decide when to advise the Secretary of State to issue more licences to allow additional companies to enter the market and I also have to decide when I should exercise my power of making determinations under the cable television companies' licences.

The key to the answer to these questions may be seen in my duty to promote the interests of customers as regards price, quality and variety of service. Trade-offs between quality and price can be difficult to judge within this framework. If an improvement in quality is likely to be achieved only by increasing competition but extra competition would be likely to bring higher prices, I have no alternative but to exercise my judgement on the merits of the price–quality trade-off. However, extra competition is not likely to lead to lower quality unless that is what customers want; consequently, a study of its likely effect on price may often be the key issue.

How am I to assess the probable effect of additional competition on price? Suppose a cable television company has applied for a determination that a reasonable demand exists for it to provide telecommunications services in a specified area. How should I decide whether or not to agree to that request? The introduction – or expansion – of competition has two main effects: the loss of economies of scale and additional incentives to become more efficient. Let us focus on these two main considerations.

Economies of scale have great importance in telecommunications. Other things being equal, it will always be cheaper to meet a given extra amount of demand by expanding an existing system rather than establishing a new one. One strong reason for this can be seen in the configuration of the network. Suppose that service in a particular area is provided from a given local exchange from which a circular cable is run to make a main artery. Spurs are run from the main artery to customers' premises. All of the cable has to be set in ducts. If local service is provided by two competing companies of about equal size, two exchanges will be required – and they will have to be connected – two arteries will have to be established and the spurs to customers' premises will benefit less often from sharing of ducts than when there is only one company. Some of the cable can be of lower capacity when there are two companies than when there is one, but doubling the capacity of cable over a given route does not come close to doubling the cost. The economies of scale may also arise in the switching and in administration and selling. These effects can be captured in a financial model of the supply of local telecommunications services.

The financial model referred to in the previous paragraph can produce an estimate of the amount by which the total costs of providing local telecommunications in an area would increase if services were provided by two competing companies instead of by a monopolist, at a given level of efficiency. However, the assumption that efficiency is unchanged is the antithesis of what one would actually expect to happen. Actually, the expectation would be that efficiency would be greater in the competitive situation. The benefits from greater efficiency must be weighed against the loss of economies of scale. If the costs of supply by two, at a given level of efficiency, are $x\%$ more than the cost of supply by one, the regulator has to ask whether or not the efficiency gains are likely to be more than $x\%$. Several sources of evidence are available to help with this question. Measures of efficiency for various overseas telephone companies can be compared with those for the existing operator. Assessment can be made of the extent to which more modern equipment is available and could be installed to produce lower running costs. The judgements required are difficult ones but they are inescapable and they are judgements of the kind that accountants can help to make.

Some people may argue that the question of the permitted extent of competition should not be a matter for regulatory judgement. They may argue that a firm which wishes to try its hand at competition should be permitted to do so. If it fails to achieve high efficiency, it is likely to fail totally but it will only have lost its own resources; if it succeeds, it may ultimately displace the previous supplier but it will have benefited the community by demonstrating a higher level of performance in the meantime. However, I believe that this would be an oversimplified view. The failure of a telephone company would produce serious economic disruption and, while no complete guarantee can exist against its occurrence, a regulator would be ill-advised to promote a situation in which it is likely to happen. Furthermore, the establishment of uneconomic competition may lead to higher prices to the customer than necessary for some considerable period of time, if not indefinitely. The regulator has no effective alternative to facing up to the difficult economic judgement of the costs and benefits of competition.

SETTING THE TERMS FOR INTERCONNECTION

A second example of an area where accounting skills are needed by a regulator concerns another aspect of competition. In telecommunications, competition can work only if a certain amount of cooperation also takes place. Mercury, the licensed competitor to British Telecom, could not expect to attract any customers unless those customers can be sure of being able to telephone British Telecom's customers. This requires the interconnection of the networks. If British Telecom could refuse to interconnect the networks, Mercury would almost certainly be unable to recruit any customers. To avoid this danger, British Telecom's licence requires it to connect its system to that of Mercury, upon application by Mercury. If the terms for the interconnection can be agreed between the two companies, that agreement is binding but, failing such agreement, Mercury can appeal to me to set down the terms and conditions. Not surprisingly, Mercury did find it necessary to obtain a ruling from me.

The licence contains quite detailed rules which I must follow in a case like this. It says, for example, that I must set down the terms which appear reasonably necessary to secure that Mercury pays to British Telecom: 'The cost of anything done pursuant to the agreement including fully allocated costs attributable to the services to be provided and taking into account relevant overheads and a reasonable rate of return on attributable assets.' I am also required to secure that the requirements of fair competition are satisfied.

Although the condition relating to the definition of cost appears to be fairly tightly drawn, accountants will recognize that there is more than one number that will satisfy the definition. The reference to fully allocated costs tells us that overheads must be included and that the price cannot be restricted to marginal or incremental cost. However, more than one method of identifying overhead costs with services is used by accountants and the different acceptable methods can produce very different results. Furthermore, the reference to 'relevant' overheads promotes further pause for thought. It should hardly be necessary to point out to the regulator that no account should be taken of the irrelevant. However, the word 'relevant' is frequently used in accounting to describe costs that are altered by a decision under consideration and this is generally a different number from that obtained by traditional systems of measuring fully allocated costs.

Another, and potentially more serious, uncertainty is the failure to distinguish between historical costs and current costs. One of the costs associated with the provision of interconnection is likely to be the depreciation of fixed assets. The current cost of these assets is likely to be very different from the historical cost – in some significant cases it may be much lower, though in other cases it may also be higher. A similar difficulty will apply to the rate of return on attributable assets. The use of historical cost would appear to lead to potentially anomalous consequences. For example, it might pay British Telecom to keep an obsolete asset in use for the service of Mercury rather than provide a modern and much cheaper equivalent. No doubt this interpretation rests on an unduly mechanistic interpretation of historical cost rules – most accountants would probably agree that the cost of an obsolete asset should be written down at least to the current cost of a modern asset with equivalent service capability, but historical cost principles for asset valuation are not well developed in accounting.

Little doubt can be felt that the current cost value is more relevant than the historical cost value. The current cost value is likely to approximate the cost that would prevail in a competitive market – the opportunity cost of using an asset. However, the measurement of current cost can be of great difficulty, particularly in telecommunications where technology is changing with great rapidity, and yet taking advantage of new technology requires adaptation of network configurations and this can be undertaken only at a limited rate. Furthermore a regulator has to consider anomalies that can arise if different concepts of cost are used for different regulatory decisions and if regulation is based on one measurement while reporting to shareholders is based on another.

Any regulatory difficulties in interpreting the rules on costing are, perhaps, lessened by the equal requirement to secure that the requirements of fair competition are satisfied. Recognition of fairness is not, of course, easy. It would seem fair if two competitors could be allowed to start in business on an equal footing. But where one competitor has an established network of very large magnitude and the other is starting from scratch, fairness is a much more elusive concept. The established operator is bound to have an advantage as far as economies of scale are concerned. However, the British regulatory system has some rules to counterbalance this effect. British Telecom is required to provide universal service – that is, service to any customer who wants it – at a price which, with a few minor exceptions, is uniform. Mercury can choose where to provide service. Consequently, Mercury can choose the routes and the locations where the cost conditions are most favourable. British Telecom also carries the lion's share of social obligations. It has to provide service in rural areas, including some public call boxes which make a loss, and it has to provide certain special services for blind and deaf people.

Whether or not the balance of these considerations is fair, and what exact computation of the costs of interconnection best complements the fairness, evidently rests on difficult judgements. However, the overall regulatory injunction to promote competition provides the key. If competition is sustainable, in the sense that both participants can make satisfactory profits, and if each has a reasonable opportunity to improve its position by superior performance, and if reason exists to think that overall efficiency gains are being made, then many of the concerns about unfairness are removed.

FAIR TRADING RULES

An example, of a rather different kind, of the pervasive importance of accounting issues in regulation, is provided by the fair trading rules. If a firm holds a position of effective monopoly power, care must be taken to ensure that it does not exploit that position directly by charging an excessive price to customers. However, monopoly power carries another indirect danger. The monopoly position can be used to support related businesses, run by the same firm, that are facing competition. The effect of this can be that, if other firms providing competition in the related activities do not also have monopoly positions to support those activities, the firm with the monopoly position can drive out competition from the related activities.

This is a real danger in telecommunications. British Telecom has monopoly power in the provision of basic telecommunications services – even though it faces competition from Mercury in some areas. It also carries on the related businesses of apparatus supply and value added services and certain other forms of communication such as radio-paging services in which it faces competition. Apparatus supply and value added services are open very widely to competition, but none of the competitors has a very significant position of dominance in basic services in the UK, and most of them do not have positions of dominance in any other business. The position in radio-paging is similar, although here competition is not open but depends on having a licence.

There are several ways in which a dominant supplier could use its position to support related businesses in an anti-competitive manner. British Telecom might – if it were permitted – charge a monopoly price on its basic services and use the profits to subsidize prices on apparatus supply, value added services or radio-paging. It would wish to do this only if it expected that the result would be to drive competitors from the market place and leave it with the prospect of earning monopoly profits later, enough to make up for the cost of cross-subsidization.

Other devices could have a similar result. The cost of internal services, used jointly by the basic business and the competing business, could be allocated unfairly so that the monopoly business bears too high a proportion. Another possibility arises when the basic business has to supply facilities which are used by both its own competing business and other competing businesses. It could charge its own business a more favourable price – or in the extreme, withhold supply altogether from others. It could also give customers preferences from its monopoly business on condition that they deal with its competing business and it could target these favours towards customers that are judged most likely to deal with competitors.

Regulation is needed to prevent these distortions of competitive markets in the interests of maintaining competition for the benefit of customers. Several kinds of regulation can make a difference. One possibility is to prevent the making of monopoly profits by controlling prices in the monopoly businesses. This approach is an important ingredient of policy in the United Kingdom. However, fair trading rules are also desirable. Our regulations contain rules against unfair cross-subsidies and they also prevent suppliers of basic services from giving undue preferences to their own businesses or to their customers.

One of the first complaints that I received on the subject of unfair competition concerned the radio-paging business. British Telecom had a very large share of the market for radio-paging but faced competition from three relatively small operators who lacked the benefit of businesses to provide basic telecommunications services in support of radio-paging. The competitors complained to me about British Telecom's behaviour and a key part of the complaint related to the practice of joint billing. British Telecom was issuing bills that covered both radio-paging and the basic telephone service: indeed, it separated the standing charge for basic telephone service (the exchange line rental) from the rental of the radio-pager only in a supplementary statement when the customers' service requirements changed; subsequently, these items were combined into one line on the bill. The companies that complained thought it was unfair that British Telecom should issue a joint bill in any circumstances because joint billing would mean that customers would tend to lose sight of the cost that they were bearing. They also asked me to investigate the apportionment of billing cost between the radio-paging business and the basic business to establish whether or not any cross-subsidization was involved.

In cases like this, the regulator faces a series of difficult issues. First, cross-subsidization is ill-defined. If a company has a basic billing system and extends the system to deal with the billing of an extra service, it is clear that the extra service should be charged at least with the incremental cost if cross-subsidization is to be avoided. However, this incremental cost is likely to be much less than the 'stand-alone cost', that is, the cost that would be incurred in providing a billing system for radio-paging separately. A regulator could not accept a charge that is below incremental cost nor insist on a charge in excess of stand-alone cost. However, the range between these two numbers is likely to be very great and accounting theory does not indicate clearly how the precise charge should be determined. Most accountants would probably say that some fair solution should be arrived at by apportioning the fixed costs of the billing system according to one of the methods in general use among accountants. However, different methods in common use can produce significantly different results.

To decide what judgement to make about such issues, a regulator must keep in mind the basic objectives of the regulatory arrangements. The key point, as I noted earlier, is to promote competition where competition benefits customers as regards price, quality or variety of service. If this judgement suggests that competition is desirable, on the grounds that potential efficiency gains outweigh losses of economies of scale (or scope), the key is to seek the adoption of a charging basis that is consistent with the continuation of competition. This might suggest that the supplier with the monopoly should charge its radio-paging business with a billing cost which is broadly the same as would be incurred by a competitor which did not have the advantage of providing basic telecommunications services but which operated with a similar level of efficiency.

My investigation of the complaint against British Telecom did not substantiate the claim that cross-subsidization was taking place. Nevertheless, I asked British Telecom to agree to produce separate bills for the radio-paging business because I was persuaded that the non-pecuniary benefits of joint billing could have the effect of distorting competition. British Telecom agreed to this suggestion. In these circumstances, my regulatory action must have increased the cost of billing to some extent − by reducing the availability of economies of scope − and action of this kind must be taken with reluctance. Nevertheless, if it contributes to the sustaining of vigorous competition it can be in the interests of customers. I might add that my investigation of these issues convinced me that greater diversity of competition in radio-paging would be beneficial and I advised the Secretary of State to issue some additional licences. He accepted this advice.

CONCLUSION

This paper has focused on a relatively narrow range of issues that have to be addressed by a regulator and to which accounting can make an important contribution. I have not discussed the important issue of how price control should be established in an area where monopoly power is pervasive, nor have I dealt with the numerous issues that are related to this broad question. I have focused, instead, on the role of the regulator in promoting competition. But this is one of the most important aspects of regulation because the promotion of competition can be seen as having a much greater potential to increase the efficiency with which services are provided to customers than efficient price control, important as this is.

Index